Blacks and Religion
Volume One

Blacks and Religion
Volume One

What did Africa contribute to the Origin of Religion?

The Equinox and the Real Story behind Easter

AND

Understanding the Book of the Dead

BY

Robin Walker

REKLAW EDUCATION LTD
London (U.K.)

First published as three e-books in 2011 and 2014 by Reklaw Education
Limited

ISBN-13: 978-1500175047

ISBN-10: 1500175048

Cover design by Robin Walker

CONTENTS

OPENING REMARKS

Early Africa and its religious heritage should be of interest to the people of modern Africa and the Black Diaspora. Unlike most academics, however, I am not anti-religious. I believe that religious ideas can be of use to modern peoples.

The key, however, is that human beings must be in control of those ideas. Those ideas cannot be in control of you.

Moreover, I believe that religious people should take Dr Edgar Ridley's critique of religious ideas seriously. He argues that there is a very thin line between religious symbolism and superstition. He believes that African symbolic thought has led to superstition in far too many cases and consequently it has become a force that has held Black people back as a people.

Even more controversially, I believe that adherents to religious traditions should always look for ways to challenge, develop and evolve those traditions. In other words, adherents to religious traditions should always be prepared to think the unthinkable. Part of the process of evolving ideas is to learn new ideas. I see this book as a basic text that may give readers many new ideas to think with.

Perhaps the word "new" is presumptuous of me. Many writers have gone before me in documenting African religious ideas. As with my previous books, I have gathered these ideas into one place.

The first part of this book began life as a Kindle e-book entitled: *What did Africa contribute to the Origin of Religion?* It addresses the Ancient and Traditional African religions and shows the common concepts that existed between them. I also show how African religious ideas evolved.

The second part of this book began life as an e-book entitled: *The Equinox and the Real Story behind Easter.* It addresses the Spring Equinox and shows that many early religions practiced similar ideas at that time of the year.

The third part of this book began life as an e-book entitled: *Understanding the Book of the Dead.* It addresses the most influential set of religious texts in the history of religion. While superficially difficult to understand, I show that the Egyptian *Book of the Dead* is not as strange or as difficult a text as it at first appears.

The final part of this book contains information about me and the lectures that I teach on these topics.

Read and enjoy

Robin Walker 2014

PART ONE

WHAT DID AFRICA CONTRIBUTE TO THE ORIGIN OF RELIGION?

INTRODUCTION

What is the world's oldest religion? What is the true religion for Black people? What was Africa's original religion?

If I earned one pound for each time I was asked these questions, I would be a wealthy man by now.

As a Black Studies lecturer of many years experience, no course module generates more controversy and debate among the adult students than religion. Everyone has something to say or contribute.

I have never presented any definitive answers to the big questions of the nature of the divine force or forces, human existence, ethics, destiny, etcetera. I have always left this up to the students to make up their own minds. What I have done, and continue to do even in this lecture-essay, is to provide adult students with the intellectual data with which to think. In doing this, I only present data that can be verified.

In teaching this module I used to recommend perhaps a dozen books for the adult students to read. Sometimes it was a page here and there. Sometimes it was a chapter. With some books, I recommended reading them from cover-to-cover. However, I never came across any self-contained book on religion that said everything I wanted it say. Consequently, I wrote this lecture-essay directly based on one of my classes so that it would say everything that I wanted it to say.

This lecture-essay traces the origin and evolution of religious ideas in early Africa. The paper also highlights parallels between the religious ideas in early Africa and the ideas believed in and practiced by traditional African societies uninfluenced by Islam or Christianity.

As with my other writings, I highlight unapologetically what Africa and Africans contributed to human culture. To this aim, I challenge both the racism and the religious bigotry that has conspired to bury the contributions of Africans to religion. Just for the record, some of the religious bigotry is even perpetuated by Black believers themselves.

I owe major intellectual debts to scholars who have gone before me in this endeavour. Chief amongst these were Dr Femi Biko, Professor Yosef ben-Jochannan, Professor John Jackson, Professor George James, Professor Charles Finch and the Reverend Mbiti.

This lecture-essay presents what is currently known about the early religious history of the human race. Yes I address questions such as: What is the world's oldest religion? However, I prefer to reframe the question as: What is the world's oldest religion that we can document? If this question interests you, read on.

There are other difficult questions such as: What is the true religion for Black people? What was Africa's original religion?

I believe that the question on the true religion for Black people cannot be answered definitively. Each person must make their own decisions. That decision, however, should be informed by verifiable knowledge. I present some of that knowledge here.

On the question of Africa's original religion, this can be answered definitively. African regions had regionally defined religions. No single tradition covered the length and breadth of the African continent. However, these religious traditions shared many common features with each other. If these features interest you, read on.

Robin Walker

June 2014

CHAPTER ONE: PROBLEMS WITH THE STUDY OF AFRICA AND RELIGION

Introduction: What is religion?

Dr Femi Biko, one of the pioneers of Black Studies teaching in the United Kingdom, has long taught that religion consists of four main elements-- Rituals, Spirituality, Ethics and Futurism.

Rituals give outward expression to a religion. Rituals are the private and public things that an adherent does to show their commitment to the religion.

Spirituality gives inward expression to a religion. Spirituality consists of the various modes and methods by which an individual seeks out a connection between him or herself, the Spirit World, and/or the Universe.

Ethics, in this context, are the moral and behavioural code of a religion. Ethics gives the adherent a rule book to follow and lays out a way of life to aspire to.

Futurism, in this context, is where a religion suggests what will happen in the future for a community at large or suggests what will happen in an individual's future. Some religions have mystics, oracles and diviners to reveal the future.

Double Standards and the Three Main Problems

Three problems have historically hampered the study of traditional African religions.

European scholars have conventionally denigrated traditional African religions in their writings. Before 1945 Christian thinking exerted a much bigger influence on European scholarship than it does today. Back then, many scholars freely denounced the beliefs and practices of non Christian peoples. Although much of European intellectual life is more secular today, the heritage of the old ideas and the accompanying bigotries and terminologies still continues to influence modern thinking on traditional African religions.

Black scholars, on the other hand, have been reluctant to study their ancient religions. Most Black people today are Christians or Muslims. Both groups traditionally took a dim view of traditional African religions. They also denounced and ostracised the adherents of these religions.

A final problem concerns the Black scholars who have attempted to 'normalise' African religions. This is where Black scholars who follow Christianity or Islam describe and interpret traditional African religions in ways that make them seem similar to Judaism, Christianity or Islam. It is true that similarities between traditional African religions and the Abrahamic faiths actually exist. The problem, however, is where the Black scholar over emphasises the similarities, blurs the differences, and thus presents a distorted picture of the traditional African religions.

To illustrate some of the points raised here, I raise questions such as:

* What is the difference between a religion and a cult?
* What is the difference between spirituality and demonology?
* What is the difference between symbols and fetishes?
* What is the difference between ancestor reverence and ancestor worship?
* What is a heathen, khaffir or an ethnic?
* What is the difference between a priest, a shaman and a witch doctor?
* What is the difference between icons and idols?

These examples demonstrate just how much Christian religious bigotry dominates intellectual discourse on religion--even in our secular age. Terms like religion, spirituality, symbols, ancestor reverence, priests and icons usually appear in positive or neutral cultural contexts. However, terms like cults, demonology, fetishes, ancestor worship, heathens, khaffirs, ethnics, shamans, witch doctors and idols usually appear in negative cultural contexts. In addition, the positive or neutral terms usually appear when writers are writing about European and Middle Eastern peoples. However, the negative terms usually appear when writers are writing about African and Native American peoples.

To add even more insult, scholars conventionally claimed that religion has undergone an intellectual evolution over the millennia from simple to complex ideas. Early and primitive peoples supposedly believed in Animism. They believed that all things had an indwelling spirit. The ancient civilisations of Egypt and India supposedly evolved a more sophisticated idea of Polytheism. They believed that there were numerous gods. Later civilisations supposedly evolved the idea of Henotheism. This belief embodies the idea of one supreme God amongst the many gods. Finally, the ancient Hebrews supposedly evolved the idea of Monotheism. This is the belief that there is one God. The monotheistic concept passed

Figure 1. The Reverend Canon John Mbiti is perhaps the most important authority on traditional African belief systems and philosophies.

into Christianity and Islam and was supposedly inherited from the Hebrews.

Why is this intellectually insulting? This model suggests that traditional African religions (and Native American religions) represent the Animistic and Polytheistic phase of intellectual evolution. It thus suggests that African thinking is basic and primitive. It also suggests that Judaism, Christianity and Islam represent the Monotheistic phase of intellectual evolution. It thus suggests that European and Middle Eastern thinking is the most advanced. It is thus pertinent to raise some troubling questions.

* Is Judaism monotheistic? How many gods are there in the Old Testament?

* What are the patron saints in Christianity?

* What is the black stone in Islam? Why do Muslims visit it?

Mainstream sources conventionally claim that Judaism is the world first monotheistic religion. Most Christian readers of the 'Old Testament' repeat this claim. However, everybody knows the passage from the Book of Genesis "Let us make man."

This raises an obvious question: Who is the "us" that is spoken of here? I am fully aware that many Christian theologians claim this is a reference

Figure 2. No one has done more to challenge intellectual prejudice against traditional African belief systems than Professor Yosef ben-Jochannan.

to God, talking to Jesus, talking to the Holy Spirit! Not only is this perspective intellectually dishonest, it is also wholly irrelevant since of the Book of Genesis is a Jewish religious text created before Christianity even existed.

In Christianity the Catholic hierarchy has deified great believers; individuals throughout its history. These deified people are called Saints and the believers can pray to them for intercessions or even miracles. Are these Saints gods?

I am aware that many Christians claim they do not subscribe to any of these Catholic ideas. However, their rejection of Catholicism is only a five hundred year old concept. Before the time of the early sixteenth century theologian, Martin Luther, these rebels against Catholicism did not even exist. It goes without saying that the Catholic hierarchy had already deified hundreds of people before the time of Martin Luther.

In Islam similar questions can be raised about the Black Stone of Mecca. During the Islamic pilgrimage, believers are required to walk around the

Black Stone seven times. What is the purpose of this ritual? To ensure that the point gets made, suppose there was a stone monument in Africa or amongst the Native Americans that believers came to visit in pilgrimages where they had a ritual that one should walk around it seven times. What would Muslims say about this? Everybody knows that such an African (or Native American) ritual would be roundly denounced as idolatry.

CHAPTER TWO: KEY FEATURES OF ANCIENT AND TRADITIONAL AFRICAN RELIGIONS

Introduction

Professor Maulana Karenga, the erudite African American author of *Introduction to Black Studies,* identified a number of common features that connect the ancient and the traditional African religions. I have added to his analysis with some of the ideas from 1992 lectures by another African American scholar Professor Charles Finch. Dr Chukwunyere Kamalu, a Nigerian philosopher, believes that African thought be divided into the Ancient, the Traditional and the Modern. He is also of the view that the Ancient and the Traditional are connected.

The Ancient Nile Valley civilisations of Sudan and Egypt represent the core of Ancient African religious thinking. This raises two problems to be addressed here.

Firstly, many people are unaware that the ancient peoples of Sudan and Egypt were in fact indigenous Black Africans. North Africa is today dominated by a people whose ancestors came from Arabia. They conquered North Africa in waves of invasion beginning in December 639 AD. Before the Arab conquest and occupation, however, the North Africans used to be Black, just like the rest of Africa. Consequently, Ancient Sudanese and Egyptian religious heritage is also the religious heritage of Black Africans and their descendents. To read more about the peopling of Ancient Egypt, I would recommend two chapters from my book *When We Ruled.* Chapters 4 and 9 give a very detailed discussion of this topic. Other good sources are Gert Muller's *Racial Unity of the Ancient Egyptians and Nubians* and his East African and *Nubian Origins of the Ancient Egyptians.*

Secondly, the Ancient Egyptians have been roundly condemned for idolatry and religious imposture by later religions. As a consequence, many Black followers of Judaism, Christianity or Islam already have prejudiced views against the Ancient Egyptians and their religious heritage. Prejudice is, of course, a barrier to learning.

The traditional African religions are the religions of early Africa that have thrived independently of Islam or Christianity. Two African tradition religions have been much written upon, the Yoruba tradition and the Dogon tradition. There are, of course, many other traditions across Africa.

Figure 3. Worship at the Yoruba Shrine of Shango.

The Yoruba religion originated in the Yoruba civilisation located in what is now Western Nigeria. Its first golden age dates back to the Kingdom of Ife. Flourishing from around 1000, the city itself dates from the sixth century AD. Writers have been impressed by the sophistication of the Yoruba divination system based on powers of four, where four to the power of four (i.e. 256) is a key number. Others have noted the complexity of the oral literature associated with it called the *Odu Ifa*. However, due to the attacks and capture of its people by slave traders in the seventeenth century, Yoruba people and religious culture have since dispersed across Brazil, Trinidad and Cuba. Thus the Yoruba tradition is the only traditional African religion that has flourished in South America, the Caribbean, as well as in Africa.

The Dogon religion flourished in the Bandiagara Cliffs of Mali. While the Dogon language is known to be very ancient, most of their religious ideas are thought to date back to the early 1200s. Through the research of Marcel Griaule, a French anthropologist and initiate into the Dogon system, the scholarly world learned about the great complexity of Dogon religious and cosmological ideas. These ideas are of scientific value to astronomers and physicists. The cosmology also marries religion and philosophy in an interesting way.

Eight Common Features of Ancient and Traditional African Religions

The traditional African religions were locally defined. Each location or territory had its own understanding of the divine force or forces. Individuals became part of the particular religious traditions depending on where they were born. No one would ever convert from one tradition to another. Nor would there ever be conflict based on one people forcibly converting another. In Ancient Egypt, the local deity of the city of Waset was Amen or Amun. The local deity of Memphis was Ptah. The local deity of Heliopolis was Ra. In the Nigeria region, the chief deity or shrine of the Igbo territories was Chukwu. The chief deity of the Yoruba territories was Oludemare.

The traditional African religions had a god head but had deification processes where human beings could be deified and become part of the god head. The Yoruba god head was Oludemare. The Zulu god head was Nkulunkulu. The Dogon god head was Amma. However, an ordinary person could become a part of the god head if the society deified him or her if their deeds were great enough. Shango is now regarded as a Yoruba deity but was originally a Yoruba king whose contribution to metallurgy ultimately led to his deification. In the Ancient Nile Valley the same thing happened to Asar or Ausar. The Greek historian, Diodorus Siculus, portrayed him as a ruler in Ancient Sudan. At a later date he was deified and became the deity of resurrection in the Nile Valley. Greek sources call him by the better known name of Osiris. At a later date, the Greeks had a deity called Dionysus which was their equivalent to Osiris. The Roman deity Bacchus is the Roman equivalent to Dionysus. It is from the Greek writers that we learn that the gods of the Ancient World were originally dead rulers in Africa.

The traditional African religions saw the divine power or powers as near (or immanent) and far (transcendent). The divine power or powers were held to be within all of us and dwell in all things. The divine power or powers are also out there somewhere in the Heavens. Consequently, intermediaries exist between the near and the far. These intermediaries were called Neters by the Ancient Egyptians, Orishas by the Yorubas, and Nummo by the Dogon.

The traditional African religions practiced reverence for the ancestors. Ancestors were revered because of their contributors to the life of the community. They were seen as guardians of tradition and life. They were also ideal intermediaries between people and divine force or forces. The chief ritual for communicating with ancestors was libations. This was where water or spirits was ritually poured onto the ground, the preserve of the ancestors.

Figure 4. Osiris, the deity of death and resurrection, holding the flail of kingly authority and the shepherd's crook. He also has handsome facial features typical of the Ancient Egyptians during this period.

Figure 5. The Greek deity Dionysus was associated with Osiris.

Figure 6. The Roman deity Bacchus was associated with Dionysus.

In traditional African societies, religion acted like social glue that bonded the society together. The Reverend Canon John Mbiti, a leading authority on traditional African religions, suggested on page 106 of his book that an African counterpart to the Déscartes dictum "I think therefore I am" would be "I am, because we are; and since we are, therefore I am". Dr Femi Biko has long taught that traditional African religions internally policed the mind. He suggests that this is a more effective way of reducing crime and building social order than the state externally policing the body. Consequently Mbiti's and Biko's explanations show why there was no division between the secular and the divine in a traditional African society. Moreover, it is likely that Atheism would have been a very rare phenomenon indeed.

In Ancient Egypt, for example, there was a concept called Ma'at. She was a deity who symbolised all that made a society run smoothly. She personified the law (and related concepts such as truth, order, balance and reciprocity) and is the direct ancestor of Libra, the European symbol that represents law, balance and justice. The key point here is that the chief role of the pharaoh of Egypt was as the guardian of Ma'at. He was not just the most powerful politician in the land. He was actually the most important religious functionary. Kings and emperors across Africa held a similarly powerful religious function.

Figure 7. The Judgment Scene from Chapter 125 of the *Book of the Dead.* In this papyrus, there are twelve people sitting in judgement. The scales represent Ma'at. The heart is weighed against the feather of Ma'at. The ideal is to not have a heavy heart. Incidentally the fact that Ma'at was believed to have had feathers raises questions of where Christians got their angel imagery from.

Figure 8. It is interesting to note that a female is still the symbol of the law. She holds the scales of justice.

Traditional African societies had a great reverence and respect for nature. They had sacred trees, sacred rivers, sacred mountains, and sacred animals. The sycamore tree became sacred to the Sudanese and Ancient Egyptian deity Hathor. The ogilisi tree was sacred to the Igbo deity Idemili. The baobab tree had a very important religious significance for the Swahili who were not Muslims. Consequently, the Swahili cities of old had two sets of religious spaces; mosques for the Muslims and the baobab trees for the Traditionalists. The Nile was sacred and associated with a deity called Hapi. He is the direct ancestor of Aquarius the water carrier. The Mountains of the Moon in the Central East Africa region was of place of great sanctity to the Ancient Egyptians. It continues to be sacred to the Maasai who regard it as the dwelling place of the deity Ngai. The Ancient Egyptians had animal and animal headed deities. Heru or Horus was a deity associated with the falcon. Sobek was associated with the crocodile. The Ancient Kushites associated the deity Apedemak with the lion.

In traditional African societies, death was considered a stage in the life cycle. Death followed the same pattern of death and rebirth as happens elsewhere throughout the cosmos. However, it was possible to achieve immortality. Traditionally, an individual achieved immortality through great deeds, through having children and relatives, and through rituals of remembrance particularly libations. Essentially, if those in the world of living continue to speak of an ancestor's name, that ancestor has become an immortal.

Finally, traditional African religions enforced a split between the esoteric and the exoteric. There was a clear religious hierarchy where the initiates were trained in various esoteric teachings. Included among these were numerology, astronomy, readings and the hard sciences. The initiated were obliged to keep their knowledge concealed from the masses of people. This is perhaps the most controversial and criticised element of traditional African religions because it meant that the masses only received a basic religious instruction. Moreover the complex symbolisms of many traditional African religions could easily be misunderstood by the masses. This could easily lead the masses into believing sheer superstition.

CHAPTER THREE: HOW DID RELIGIOUS IDEAS EVOLVE?

Introduction

A number of scholars have attempted to trace the origin and evolution of religious ideas. Two Black scholars have used their findings to challenge the religious bigotry that has traditionally dominated discourse on Africa and religion. They have also used their findings to wake the Black Communities up. Professor John Jackson, an African American academic, wrote *Pagan Origins of the Christ Myth* in 1941. He also wrote *Man, God, and Civilization* in 1972, one of the glories of African American scholarship. The Ethiopian Egyptologist, Professor Yosef ben-Jochannan, wrote the incomparable *African Origins of the Major Western Religions* in 1970. Jackson's and ben-Jochannan's research influenced another Black writer, Charles Finch, to enter the fray. He wrote *Echoes of the Old Darkland* in 1991.

Figure 9. Gerald Massey.

This research has led many in the Black Communities to re examine earlier research on the origin and evolution of religion that has either been overlooked by mainstream scholarship or has been suppressed by that scholarship. Two earlier scholars whose work has proved fruitful in this discussion were Gerald Massey and his student Dr Albert Churchward. African American scholar Professor St Clair Drake has correctly pointed out major methodological problems with Massey and Churchward's scholarship. Wikipedia, at the time of me writing this lecture-essay, has denounced their research as pseudohistory.

My position is unless you have written the book yourself it is unlikely that you will agree with all of its contents. A writer can present information that is false. Another can present information that is basically true but has based it on no evidence. Yet another writer can present information that is true but has based it on poor evidence. Then you have writers who present conclusions that are false but have presented fruitful evidence. In other words, a book does not have to be accepted whole or rejected whole. It is always possible to pull sense out of any source--if you know what you are doing.

The Evolution of Religious Ideas

Gerald Massey in his 1907 masterpiece *Ancient Egypt: The Light of the World* raised the question: Did man create God in his own image?

After addressing this question, Gerald Massey in the first chapter of his book concluded "no."

Humans originally conceived of the God concept as "super-human types". Massey used the word type in the same way that social and behavioural scientists use the related word archetype. These types represented super human powers and were thus given animal imagery. Among these types was the pregnant hippo, the panting lion, the evolving tadpole (frog), etcetera. The pregnant hippo was large, impressive and was about to give birth to new life. The panting lion was dramatic and powerful. The evolving tadpole symbolised developmental change as one moves through different stages of the life cycle.

At a later date or cultural stage, other types came from the elemental powers of darkness and light. The Moon was associated with darkness. The Sun was associated with light.

Massey concluded that the anthropomorphic deities of the much later religions evolved at a much later intellectual stage.

Professor Charles Finch in his book and lectures shows that the original mother goddesses were images derived from nature. Like Massey, he argues that prehistoric peoples preserved their belief systems in mythology and legends. By looking at the elaborate religion of the Ancient Egyptians, Finch believes that this ancient religion has preserved the mythology and legends of even older peoples from inner Africa. Since the Ancient Egyptians had animal and animal headed deities, this may well have indicated that the early peoples of inner Africa venerated the divine power or powers using the imagery of animals--the super human types.

How long ago was this? The chief problem with attempting to write history of the prehistoric era is that prehistory means before the era of written documents. Written documents appear for the first time 5900 BC in a part of Africa, 3300 BC in a part of Western Asia, 1200 BC in a part of the Americas, 750 BC in a part of Southern Europe. All human achievements before these dates were prehistoric. Anatomically modern humans have been in existence for 200,000 years. Consequently, at some point between 200,000 years ago and 5900 BC early Africans conceived of some of the religious ideas identified by Massey and also Finch. Some of these ideas were preserved in the religion of the Ancient Egyptians.

Professor Finch wrote the following that outlines his methods for reconstructing the religious history during this period when there were no written documents:

> Is it possible to probe into the evolution of human consciousness in the same fashion as we do human biological evolution, particularly during the period we call the Upper Paleolithic, c. 40-10,000 B.C., when African *Homo sapiens sapiens* was sowing the seeds of modern culture? To the extent we are able to trace the history of the human mind, we must rely on material ordinarily considered "non-historical," i.e., folk customs, myths, religious symbols, and language. Most historians shun the use of such materials because it is difficult to impose rigor upon them and they are usually impossible to date precisely. Still, such material has provided a wealth of valuable information.

Emphasising this point, Professor Finch wrote:

> Little in the human experience is totally lost; its deposits are left in language, myth, history, religion, architecture, literature, art, and the psyche itself.

Professor Finch believes that Ta-Urt which is imaged as a pregnant hippo and represented Great Mother Earth was the oldest deity known to us moderns. Countless deities may well have been conceived of by humans before Ta-Urt but of these there are no records whatsoever. There are no

Figure 10. The deity Ta-Urt.

documents, artefacts or surviving mythology or legends. Moving from the unknown to the known, Ta-Urt may well represent the beginnings of religious prehistory.

Finch suggests that as we have the earth floating around the Nu or heavens, a hippo becomes a powerful symbol representing Great Mother Earth but this time floating around the swamps of inner Africa. She is not only large and impressive. Representative of the earth, she sustains life. She is also pregnant and is therefore about to create life. What an awesome image of the divine power or powers!

Finch suggests that later images of the divine power or powers came from trees. The branches of trees represented protection and the fruit represented sustenance. The Ancient Sudanese and Egyptian goddess Het-Heru also known as Hathor was associated with the sycamore tree. Gert Muller in *East African and Nubian Origins of the Ancient Egyptians* states that the sycamore tree did not originally grow in Egypt. It originated in inner Africa where it was carried north from Central Africa by ancestors of the Ancient Egyptians who brought it to Egypt. At a later date, the Igbos of what is now Eastern Nigeria associated their goddess Idemili with the ogilisi tree.

Figure 11. The deity Hathor as a human female with cow's ears. She has exquisite broad features typical of Ancient Egyptian women of this period.

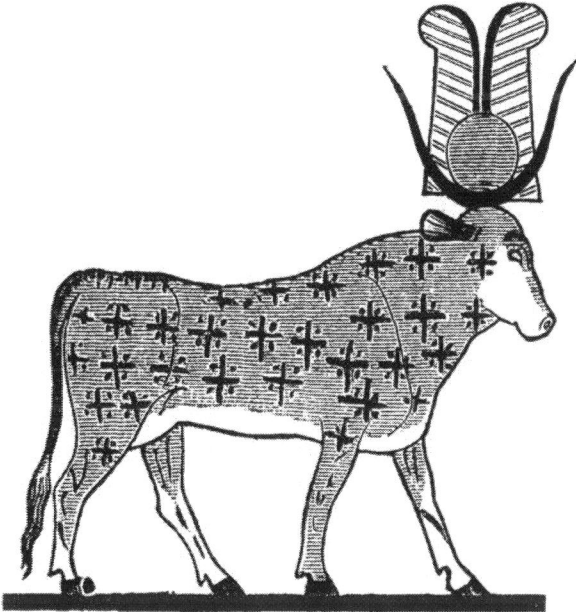

Figure 12. The deity Hathor as a cow. She has a moon disk above her head. Is this the origin of the halo?

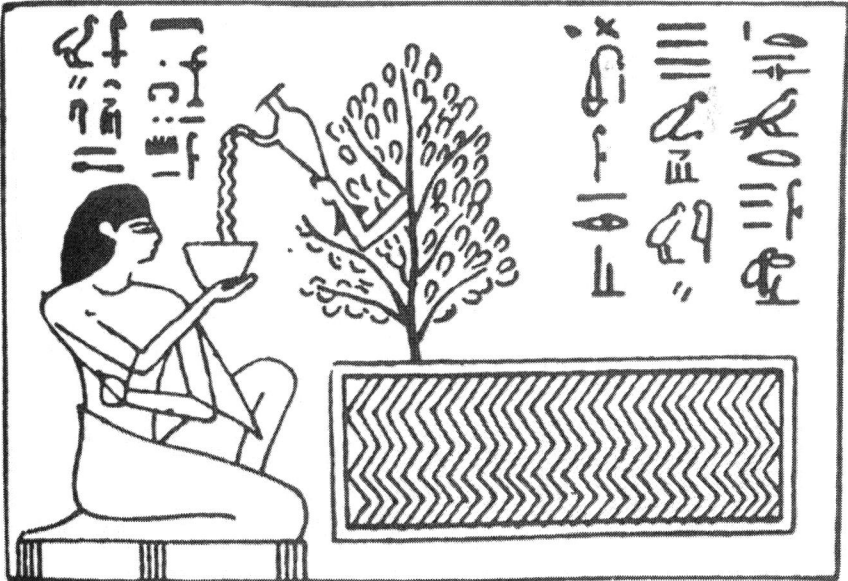

Figure 13. The deity Hathor as a sycamore tree.

Figure 14. The Greek deity Aphrodite was associated with Hathor.

At a later date still, the divine power was imaged as the moon. The lunar cycle of the moon is approximately the same length as a woman's menstrual cycle. Consequently, the moon was considered female by many religious traditions. The goddess Hathor was associated with the moon. At a later date the goddess Aset or Auset was also associated with the moon. This deity is better known under the Greek name Isis. Incidentally, Hathor is the same deity adored by the Greeks under the name Aphrodite. Isis was adored by the Ancient Greeks under the name Demeter.

Beyond making the vague suggestion that the age of the moon goddesses must have taken place somewhere between 200,000 years ago and 5900 BC, archaeologists have more specific evidence from the Lebombo Bone. This South African artefact, dated at 37,000 years old, has a series of notches carved into it that is almost certainly a lunar calendar. It is therefore possible that the age of the moon goddesses may date back originally to this kind of period.

The next stage in the evolution of religion might have been the female deities that came about as a result of the deification process. Early prehistoric societies were certainly matrilineal and very likely matriarchal in character. It is likely that communities consisted almost entirely of women and their children. Fatherhood may well have been unrecognised. Moreover, men would have had no ability to limit women's access to resources as populations remained small and resources were relatively plentiful. Consequently, men would have had no power to enforce patriarchal marriage.

Consequently the evidence of goddesses such as Isis associated with corn, Neith associated with both weaving and warfare using the bow and arrow, and Shesheta associated with writing suggests that women pioneered these things. Thus a woman invented farming and was later deified under the name of Aset or Isis. Another invented weaving. Another invented warfare using bows and arrows. Perhaps these inventions were the ideas of several women. Whichever be the case the mythologies surrounding these women merged into a set of mythologies surrounding one woman who was deified as Nit or Neith. Incidentally, at a much later date Neith was adored by the Ancient Greeks as Athena. Finally some woman presumably pioneered the use of writing. She was deified under the name of Shesheta.

It is worth pointing out, as an aside, that in Ice Age Europe while populations remained small, resources were always scarce due to the ubiquity of ice. Consequently, men in Europe were able to limit women's access to resources and become the gatekeepers to that access. Thus Ice Age European men were able to enforce patriarchal marriage well before men in tropical climates were able to do this.

Several writers suggest that the next stage in the evolution of religious ideas and human culture was due to the influence of Totemism and Taboo. Totemism is the idea that your clan descends from a particular animal or plant totem that ultimately became your clannic identity and clannic name. Consequently, people took their clan name from a type of plant or an animal and may also have developed a mythology to show how their clan descended from that plant or animal!

Eventually, however, these prehistoric societies began to see the totems as items that are taboo. This meant that it was forbidden for members of the clan to consume these plant or animal products. However, people from other clans may not have the same taboo against consuming these totemic products. Consequently, people would trade products that they considered taboo with other peoples who did not consider these products taboo. This process led to the birth of economics and ultimately to the birth of civilisation! The Kingdom of Ta-Seti was the first known state in history. I controversially date the first pharaohs of Ta-Seti to approximately 5900 BC.

The next stage in the evolution of religious ideas was the appearance of male deities. Fatherhood became generally recognised and human family structures changed to include men in the family unit. Since civilisation is associated with city living and the accompanying population explosions, the larger populations placed a strain on the available resources allowing resources to be rationed for the first time. If men could control access to these resources, this would have raised their power and thus their desirability to women. Consequently, men not only entered the family unit, but they entered the unit as its head. This began the era of patriarchy.

One of the first documented male deities was Set. Other early male deities that appeared in the Nile Valley pantheon were Asar or Ausar (better known as Osiris), Heru (better known as Horus), Atum-Ra, Ptah and Tehuti (better known as Thoth). Most of these deities were associated with the Sun. However, Osiris and Thoth, for some reason, were associated with the Moon. Incidentally, Ptah was later adored by the Greeks as Hephaestos. He was later adored by the Romans as Vulcan. Thoth was later adored by the Greeks as Hermes and by the Romans as Mercury.

The next development of religious ideas was the birth of scripture. The oldest known religious writings in the world were the *Pyramid Texts* written during the time of Egyptian Pharaoh Unas of the Fifth Dynasty. I controversially date him to between 4435 and 4402 BC. The *Pyramid Texts* contain a very male-dominated account, typical of later religions.

CHAPTER FOUR: THE NILE VALLEY COSMOLOGY

Introduction

The cosmology of the Nile Valley Africans from the Old Kingdom Period to the Kushite Period has been much discussed. Five important Black scholars have written learnedly on these cosmological systems.

Professor George G. M. James, the brilliant Guyanese philosopher, described these systems in his classic *Stolen Legacy* in 1954. In the subtitle to the book James declared *The Greeks Were Not the Authors of Greek Philosophy, But the People of North Africa, Commonly Called the Egyptians.* However, his account, while basically accurate, did not quote directly from Ancient Egyptian sources. Instead, he relied on what Masonic writers claimed the Ancient Egyptians believed. This oversight allowing critics of James to falsely claim that his account of the Egyptian cosmology was bogus. Moreover, James made errors in his interpretation of the cosmology by using a Greek concept called dialectics to interpret the Egyptian ideas. This error allowed critics to claim that James exaggerated the extent to which the Greek ideas resembled those of the Egyptians.

Professor Jacob Carruthers, an African American Egyptologist, also wrote learnedly on the Nile Valley cosmological systems in his *Essays in Ancient Egyptian Studies.* His interpretation is a clear advance compared to the work of Professor James. Unfortunately, however, even Carruthers accused James of presenting a Greek tainted version of the Egyptian belief system.

Professor Cheikh Anta Diop, the great Senegalese scholar, wrote *Civilisation or Barbarism* in 1990. He divides the cosmological systems into four different schools of thought. He designated one school as the Hermopolitan, another as Heliopolitan, another as Memphite and the last school as Theban. All these systems were named after the Egyptian cities where each school originated.

Father Innocent Onyewuenyi, a Nigerian philosopher, wrote *The African Origin of Greek Philosophy* in 1993. Unlike James and Diop, he quotes directly from the Ancient Egyptian sources and demonstrates that James was basically correct. Professor Onyewuenyi quotes liberally from the

Pyramid Texts, Coffin Texts, Ramesside Stela, Book of the Dead, Leiden Papyrus, Amarna Letters and the *Hymn to Aten.*

Finally, Professor Théophile Obenga, the Congolese Egyptologist, historian and philosopher, wrote *African Philosophy: The Pharaonic Period* in 2004. Unlike the previous scholars, he has translated the primary Egyptian source documents himself and has published the hieroglyphics, his translations, and commentaries upon them.

In writing my account, I have brought together the findings of all five scholars. Unlike Professor Diop, I agree with Professor James as seeing the cosmological systems as one coherent model and not as three or four different schools of thought. Secondly, when we remove the Greek dialectical interpretations from the Nile Valley cosmologies as Carruthers has done, the result shows even more convincingly the extent to which ancient Greek thinkers borrowed from Nile Valley ideas! Professor James's critics have, of course, remained silent on this demonstrable fact.

The Cosmology or Cosmological Systems

The first part of the cosmology outlines the dimensions and potential of all that will come into being. Other writers present this as the Hermopolitan cosmology. These principles were presented as male female pairs. As male and females they represent potential, just as a man and a woman have a potential ... to reproduce.

The first pair are Nun and Naunet which mean the Primeval Waters and represent Nothingness. The second pair are Huh and Hauhet which represent Boundlessness or Infinity. The third pair are Kuk and Kauket which represent Darkness. The fourth pair are Amen and Amenet which represent The Hidden. These are all potentials.

When these couples reproduce, Nun and Naunet produce Things, Huh and Hauhet produce Finiteness, Kuk and Kauket produce Light and Amen and Amenet produce Visibility.

The second part of the cosmology is the creation from Nun. Other writers call this the Heliopolitan cosmology. Beginning with the Primeval Waters, formless, uncreated, and rich with potential, the deity Ptah emerges from the waters in the form of a hill and represents stability. In Egyptian architecture, the shapes of the Pyramids were symbolical of Ptah emerging as a hill. Standing on the hill is the deity Atum-Ra who executes the work of creation. He is sometimes considered the sun or solar fire. He is also depicted as a man. Atum-Ra creates two elements Shu (air) and Tefnut

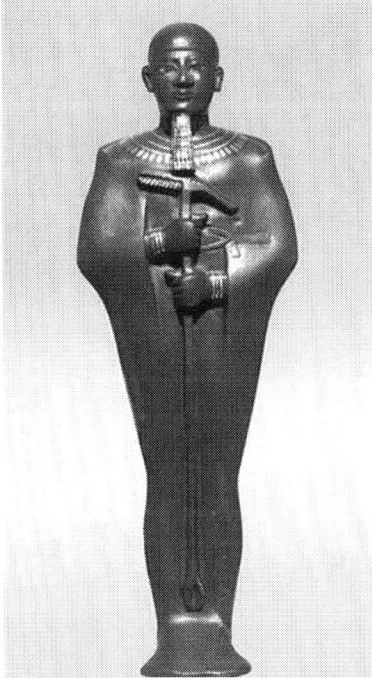

Figure 15. The deity Ptah in his typical pose and attitude.

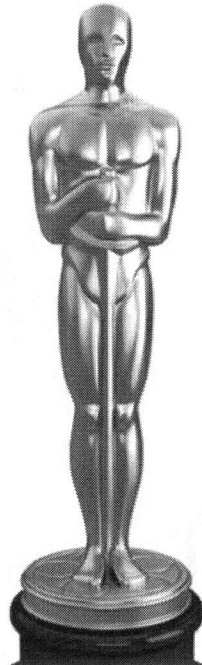

Figure 16. It is no secret that Hollywood has continued to make extensive use of Ancient Egyptian imagery. This is the trophy of the Oscars. Compare with the pose and attitude of Ptah.

(water). They are also a male female pair. Shu and Tefnut reproduce and give birth to two more elements Geb (earth) and Nut (sky). Professor Obenga quotes from the *Pyramid Texts* a passage that clearly suggests that Nut is also fire. Finally, Geb and Nut, another male female pair, reproduce and give birth to Osiris, Isis, Set and Nephthys. Osiris and Isis symbolised the positive qualities that were passed on to all human beings. Set and Nephthys symbolised negative qualities that were also passed on to all human beings.

The third part of the cosmology describes how Ptah's power and spirit runs through all deities and the lives of people, animals and things. Other writers call this the Memphite cosmology. Ptah is the God of Gods, thought, creative utterance and power, principle of order and form, and the divine artificer and potter.

The influence of these cosmological ideas on the Ancient Greeks from between the seventh and the fourth centuries BC cannot be overstated. Thales taught that water is the source of all things. Anaximander believed that the origin of all things is the infinite or the unlimited. Anaximenes held that all things originated from air. Heraclitus taught that fire is the underlying element in the universe. He also believed that divine law and universal reason runs through all things.

CHAPTER FIVE: THE STORY OF ISIS AND OSIRIS

Introduction

Isis and Osiris were very important deities in the Ancient Egyptian belief system. However, no complete account of their story has survived in indigenous Egyptian sources. There are allusions to their story carved on temple walls, bits and pieces in the *Book of the Dead,* etcetera, but no full account. Consequently, scholars use Plutarch's *Concerning the Mysteries of Isis and Osiris* for the core of the story and they supplement it with the evidence from the Egyptian wall carvings and the other documents. Plutarch himself was an ancient Roman scholar. He stated that the primary source he consulted for his account came from an Ancient Egyptian historian and high priest Manetho. The whole of the Plutarch document is in G. R. S. Mead's invaluable 1906 work *Thrice Greatest Hermes: Volume One,* pages 255 to 366.

Another important European writer was Macrobius. A Roman scholar of the fourth century, he is a key source of the Solar Myth theory. He documents the fact that the deities of the ancient world associated with the sun, were commemorated at the same time in late December. In his own words: "These differences of age refer to the sun which seems to be a babe at the Winter Solstice, as the Egyptians represent him in their temples on a certain day; that being the shortest day, he is then supposed to be small and an infant."

The Story of Isis and Osiris

Professor John Jackson, author of *Man, God, and Civilization,* pages 105 to 107, presented a summary of the story which is based on Plutarch's account and supplemented by many other sources, which I have extracted below:

> Osiris, it is said, withdrew from the realm of the gods and became an earthy king. He found the Egyptians savages and conferred upon them the blessings of civilization; since the inhabitants of the Nile land had been cannibals before the earthly pilgrimage of Osiris. Queen Isis found barley and wheat growing wild on the banks of the great river, and King Osiris introduced the cultivation of

these grains among the people, who then eschewed cannibalism and accommodated themselves to a diet of corn. Osiris was the original gatherer of fruit from trees; he trained the creeping vines to twine themselves around poles and was the first to tread the grapes. The good king then turned over the government of Egypt to his queenly wife, Isis, while he travelled over the world distributing the blessings of agriculture and civilization to all mankind. In lands where the soil and climate did not permit the culture of wine, Osiris taught the people to brew beer from barley. On returning to Egypt, the benevolent monarch, on account of the blessings he had diffused among men, was recognized as a god and thus was worshipped by a grateful populace. But, unfortunately, Osiris had a wicked and jealous brother named Set; and the evil Set, with seventy-two accomplices, plotted the death of Osiris. Craftily, Set obtained the measurements of his brother's body and constructed a coffer of attractive design and of exactly the same dimensions. Then at a banquet, when drinking and revelry were at their height, the wily Set brought in his coffer and offered to make a present of it to anyone whose body would fit into it exactly. All present, with the exception of Osiris, tried out the coffer and none of them fitted into it; then Osiris lay in it, and it fitted him exactly. Immediately the conspirators slammed down the lid of the chest, fastened it with nails, sealed it with molten lead, and then hurled it into the Nile ... The widowed Isis soon thereafter went into exile in the papyrus swamps of the Delta, and there she gave birth to a son, the younger Horus. Meanwhile, the floating coffin of Osiris had drifted into the Mediterranean Sea and was finally washed up on the coast of Phoenicia. Here a mysterious tree sprang up and enclosed the chest in its trunk. The local king saw the tree and so admired it that he had it cut down and fashioned into a pillar for his palace at Byblos. Isis wandered over the face of the earth seeking the body of her dead husband, and eventually arrived at Byblos. After splitting the tree pillar and retrieving the coffer, Isis swathed the pillar in linen, poured ointment over it and presented it to the King of Byblos. Then the sacred pillar was installed in a Temple of Isis, where it was thereafter worshipped by the natives of Byblos. The body of Osiris was taken back to Egypt by Isis, and there hidden in a secret place. But one ill-fated evening while Set was hunting for boars by the light of the full moon, he chanced to discover the hidden chest. Proceeding to open it, he took the body of Osiris and chopped it into fourteen pieces, which he scattered all over the land of Egypt. Isis later made a search and found all the parts of Osiris except one. Each fragment was buried by Isis where she found it, and that is why so many cities of Egypt claimed possession of the grave of Osiris. The missing part of Osiris was the phallus, so Isis made an image of it for use in the religious festivals of the Egyptians ... The story of Osiris has a happier ending in some of the native versions which supplement the account written by Plutarch. We are told that, after Isis had discovered the body of Osiris and collected the fragments thereof, she and her sister Nephthys sat down and wept. This lament was heard by the sun god Ra, who, moved by compassion, dispatched help from heaven the jackal-headed god Anubis. This divinity, with the help of Horus, Isis, Nephthys, and the ibis-headed Thoth, re-assembled the body of Osiris from the numerous fragments, then the gods made a mummy of the corpse. Isis, who by good fortune was fitted out with wings, fanned the mummy with them. The breath of

Figure 17. Statue of the Goddess Isis and her son Horus.

life returned to Osiris and, in consequence, his resurrection from the dead occurred. He then betook himself to the other world to reign in perpetuity as King of the Dead. His son Horus, having grown to manhood, became a king and ruled on earth. Later on, he became the third person in the great Egyptian trinity of Osiris, Isis, and Horus. The resurrection of Osiris is pictured in a series of bas-reliefs on the walls of his temple of Denderah. First we see the dead god as a mummy lying on his bier. Then he rises up gradually. Finally, we see him standing erect between the guardian wings of Isis, who stands behind him. In front of the risen god is a male figure who holds up to his sight a crux ansata [i.e. an ankh], the symbol of life eternal.

A number of scholars have analysed portions of this story. Gerald Massey wrote one of the most detailed analyses to date in his *Ancient Egypt: The Light of the World* of 1907. The Reverend Charles H. Vail wrote *The World's Saviours* in 1913. Dr Albert Churchward wrote *The Origin and Evolution of Religion* in 1924. Finally, Professor John Jackson wrote *Pagan Origins of the Christ Myth* in 1941.

These writers found that Horus was known as the word. He was the road. He was the lamb. He was doing his father's work. In his solar aspect, he was born on the twenty fifth of December. The sculptures show him in his mother's arms wearing the Pharaonic headdress indicating that he was born a king. There is considerable mystery over his life between the ages of

Figure 18. First two scenes from the Luxor Nativity from the time of Amenhotep III (1538-1501 BC).

Figure 19. More from the Luxor Nativity scene.

twelve and thirty. He was baptised aged thirty in the River Nile. He was also an incarnation of his father.

Isis was the divine mother who conceived miraculously. One of her names meant "the beloved". In the Ancient Egyptian tongue, this is rendered as "Meri" or "Merry".

Osiris died and resurrected. His backbone became the Djed, the very symbol of resurrection. According to Massey, his mummified body became the Karast. In Chapter 125 of the *Book of Dead,* he is shown as the Judge of the Souls of the Dead in the Hall of the Two Truths. He was considered the father of Horus. He was also the shepherd of men holding his shepherd's crook.

Due to his association with the moon, he was cut into fourteen pieces. This is a reference to the moon waxing and waning fourteen times in a lunar month. His death and resurrection is also associated with the moon. At the end of a lunar month, the moon 'dies'. It disappears for two nights. On the third night, it is 'reborn' since it reappears on that night.

The Temple of Amenhotep III (1538-1501 BC) has bas reliefs showing the birth of Amenhotep III as Horus. The Pharaohs saw themselves as the incarnation of Horus and in many Pharaonic inscriptions the pharaoh is referred to as "the Horus".

In the first relief, Thoth appears to Amenhotep's mother as Mut-Em-Ua (i.e. the Mother of the One) to announce to her that she will give birth.

In the second relief, Hathor and Kneph hold up ankhs to Mut-Em-Ua's nose. She is depicted with the enlarged stomach of pregnancy. Hathor is the goddess mentioned earlier. Kneph is the Holy Spirit. The Ankh is the key of life. This suggests that Mut-Em-Ua has breathed in the key of life and has been influenced by the Holy Spirit. This is the cause of the pregnancy.

In the third relief, the adoration of the child is depicted. In the second row, right hand side of the image are three humans holding up ankhs in their right hands. They have objects in their left hands that they are offering to the child. Who are these three people? What are these objects they are offering?

Clearly the birth of Amenhotep III is symbolic of the birth of Horus. Thoth announced the birth of Horus to Isis. Hathor and Kneph appear to Isis with ankhs which results in a pregnancy. Finally there is the adoration of the mother and child replete with three people bringing gifts.

CHAPTER SIX: THE NILE VALLEY RELIGION

Introduction

There is much that remains unknown about the Ancient Egyptian religion. Most readers find the *Book of the Dead* to be mumbo-jumbo. When properly understood, the book describes the journey and trials of the dead person's soul as it travels through the Netherworld before emerging triumphant (hopefully) in the Hall of the Two Truths. It can also be seen as a very rich adventure story that has influenced all subsequent adventure stories. One could even see it as a horror story that has influenced all subsequent horror stories.

Is the journey in the *Book of the Dead* an actual account of what the Ancient Egyptians literally believed happened to a dead person's soul? Is the journey symbolic of the trials and tribulations that challenge ordinary people living in the here and now? Is it a combination of the two? So far, scholars have avoided these questions.

Moreover scholars do not seem to know how the Ancient Egyptians engaged with the divine force or forces. Did they pray? If so, how? Did they meditate? Did they engage with the divine through physical movement (as in Yoga)? Did they make sacrifices? If so, how did it work? Did they attempt to get into trance states? Did they use alcohol or mind altering substances? Did they use music? Did they use dance? Did they combine numerous methods? Again, scholars have avoided these questions.

The only issue that writers seem to have agreed upon is that the Egyptian temples may well have been places that kept the masses of people out. The general public were not privy to the goings on in the temples. If this interpretation is correct, this raises another question: How did the masses practice the religion?

What do we know about the Nile Valley Religion?

Chapter 125 of the *Book of the Dead* shows that the ultimate aim of the Ancient Egyptian religion was to receive a favourable judgement in the Hall of the Two Truths in the Netherworld. In the Judgement scene, the soul of the dead individual enters the Hall of the Two Truths. His or her heart is weighed against the feather of Ma'at in a scale or balance. If the person had a heavy heart that tipped the feather, this was evidence that he or she led a sinful life. That person would suffer the ultimate punishment of being eaten by the Devourer of the Unjustified. They thus became known as the Twice Dead. If the heart was as light as a feather, the person received a favourable judgement. Standing near the scales was Thoth. He had a written record of that person's life.

Also in the Hall of the Two Truths were 42 beings also in judgement. The *Papyrus of Ani,* the best studied version of the *Book of the Dead,* has 12 beings sitting in judgement. The soul of the dead individual had to name each of these judges and state a declaration of innocence which indicated that the individual keep the laws of Ma'at. That is, he or she should state which sin they took responsibility for NOT having committed. Addressed to the first judge, the individual said: "I have not done iniquity". To the second judge, he or she said: "I have not committed robbery with violence." To the third, he or she said: "I have done violence to no man." To the fourth, he or she said: "I have not committed theft." To the fifth, he or she said: "I have not slain man or woman." In total there were 42 such declarations. Some writers call them the Declarations of Innocence. Others call them the Negative Confessions.

In the *Papyrus of Ani,* Horus is shown taking Ani by the hand to meet his father Osiris. This probably symbolises that the way to the father is through the son.

Gerald Massey wrote of an important event in the Ancient Egyptian calendar called The Feast of Osiris-Seker-Ptah. He states that the Egyptians celebrated 10 mysteries in the month of Choiak which is November 27 to December 26. The biggest of these mysteries was the Sixth Mystery on 22 December. There is an inscription referring to this festival at the Temple of Medinet Habu. This institution required 3,694 loaves of bread, 600 cakes, 905 jugs of beer, and 33 jars of wine for the feast. Following this was a fist fight which symbolised the death of the law just as Osiris died. Following this was the Feast of the Erection of the Djed Pillar. This symbolised Osiris rising again and re-establishing stability. Law and order had returned.

The *Book of the Dead* was one of a number of sacred Egyptian texts. The correct name for the book was *Peret Em Heru* which means *Coming Forth By Day.* This is a direct reference to the soul of a dead individual coming alive each morning and having freedom of movement to do what it liked but it must rejoin the mummified body of the dead person each night. Dr

Figure 20. Pharaoh Seti I raising the Djed pillar.

Albert Churchward quotes a passage from Chapter 18 of a *Book of the Dead* papyrus which declares: "Make the word of Osiris truth against his enemies. Raise up the [Djed] which image the resurrection of the god, let the mummy type of the eternal be once more erected as the mainstay and divine support of all."

This passage explicitly states that the adherent to the religion must make the word of Osiris truth against his enemies. It also states that raising the Djed pillar represents the resurrection of Osiris. Finally, it states that the resurrection of Osiris is the divine support for everyone.

The other sacred texts were the *Book of Gates* and the *Book of Breathings*. There were also wisdom texts such as the *Maxims of Ptahhotep.* An exquisite work of moral philosophy, some writers speak of this text as the oldest complete book in the world. Finally, there are texts that are believed to be hymns. Perhaps the most famous of these was the text associated with Pharaoh Akhenaten called the *Hymn to Aten.*

CHAPTER SEVEN: THE CONCEPTION OF THE SELF

Introduction

What are the elements that make up a human being? What is that makes you ... you? The French founder of modern European philosophy, Rene Déscartes, suggested there were two elements--mind and body. A human, according to him, had a metaphysical aspect and a physical aspect. In this section, I pose the question: Did the Ancient Egyptians pioneer this discussion thousands of years before Déscartes?

Figure 21. Rene Déscartes.

Two Black scholars have given this question due prominence. Professor Na'im Akbar, a prominent African American psychologist, wrote an exquisite essay called *Nile Valley Origins of the Science of the Mind* which appeared in the book *Egypt: Child of Africa* in 1994. Dr Chukwunyere Kamalu, a Nigerian philosopher, explicitly addressed this issue in his profound book *Person, Divinity and Nature* of 1998.

The Multiple Selves in the Book of the Dead

Professor Na'im Akbar believes that the different spiritual concepts mentioned throughout the *Book of the Dead* also have relevance in psychology. He argues that the Ancient Egyptian use of these concepts indicate what he calls the *Nile Valley Origins of the Science of the Mind*. He thus suggests that the science of the mind, i.e. psychology, has its origins in the *Book of the Dead*. Moreover, the spiritual concepts mentioned therein are also psychological concepts. Among these were the *ka* (spirit), *ba* (soul), *ab* (heart), *ren* (name), *khat* (body), *kaibit* (shadow), *sah* (spiritual body), and *akh* (soul of the spiritual body). If Akbar is correct about this, it means that the Ancient Egyptian thinkers who wrote the *Book of the Dead* conceived of a human being as being a cluster of selves. Akbar himself has written a book showing his own conception of a human being called *The Community of Self.*

In truth, no scholar knows for certain what the spiritual/psychological concepts in the *Book of the Dead* means. However, they CERTAINLY show that the Ancient Egyptians thought that a human being was rather more than just mind and body. Only the details are up for debate. Professor Akbar presents the interpretations of different scholars for comparison.

According to Gerald Massey, the concepts are *ka* (formal structure that would return to the elements), *ba* (breath of life), *khaba* (veil of the vital principle that produced emotion and motion), *abku* (seat of intelligence and mental perception), *seb* (self-creative power of the human being that manifests at puberty), *putah* (intellectual soul), and the *atmu* (eternal soul). Professor Akbar compiled this data from a lecture Massey wrote on this subject in 1900.

According to Sir E. A. Wallis Budge, the greatest of the English Egyptologists, the concepts are *ka* (double or inner self), *ba* (a combination of intelligence and spirit that leave the body after death), *khabit* (shadow), *hati* (conscience), *sahu* (spiritual body), and *khu* (the pure spirit of Horus). Professor Akbar compiled this data from Budge's classic 1913 edition of the *Book of the Dead* and the *Papyrus of Ani*.

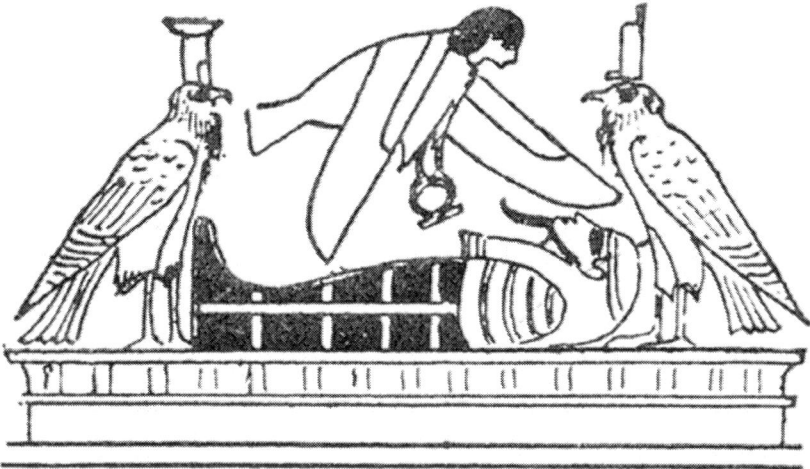

Figure 22. The *ba* depicted in an Egyptian papyrus hovering over the mummy of a deceased individual.

According to Professor George G. M. James, the concepts are *ka* (abstract personality), *ba* (the heart-soul that dwells in the ka), *kaibit* (shadow), *ab* (the heart), *khat* (the physical body), *sahu* (body in which the *khu* or spiritual self dwells), and the *khu* (spiritual soul which is immortal). Professor Akbar compiled this data from James' classic *Stolen Legacy* of 1954.

According to Isha Schwaller de Lubicz, a popular French Egyptologist, the concepts are *ka* (formal element which gives form to substance and creates matter), *ba* (the most spiritual element in man that links him to the Creator), *khabit* (astral or etheric body, ghost or shadow), *inferior ka* (inherited characteristics of psychological consciousness), and *divine ka* (spiritual witness). Professor Akbar compiled this data from the de Lubicz book *The Opening of the Way* of 1981.

The Multiple Selves in Other African Traditions

Dr Chukwunyere Kamalu on pages 53 to 62 of his book suggests that in many African traditions a person is viewed as a cluster of selves. In his own words:

> THE DESTINY OR SPIRITUAL DOUBLE Variously known as *Ka* (ancient Egyptian), *Chi* (Igbo of Nigeria), *Ori* (Yoruba of Nigeria), *Kra* (Asante of Ghana), *Kla* (Ga of Ghana), *Ehi* (Bini of Nigeria), *Se* (Fon of Benin), *Ido* (Kuba

of Zaire), etc. The concept of the spiritual double is so called because in many African cultures this self is thought to have two parts or aspects: one residing in the person's body, whilst simultaneously, the other resides in the "heavens" or the invisible realm ... THE SOUL OR BREATH Variously known as *Ba* (ancient Egyptian), *Emi* (Yoruba), aspects of *Obi* and *Chi* (Igbo), *Se* (Fon), *N'shanga* (Bambala), *Mophuphu* (Kuba), *Kra* (Asants), etc. This aspect of the person is the individual's life-force or animating principle ... THE HEART Variously known as *Ib* (ancient Egyptian), *Obi* (Igbo), *Emi* (Yoruba), etc. This would appear to be the aspect of the person which thinks and feels ... ANCESTRAL GUARDIAN Variously represented as an aspect of *Ba* (ancient Egyptian), *Mogya Ntoro* (Asante), *Ori* (Yoruba), *Eke* (Igbo), *Joto* (Fon), *Ehi* (Bini), etc. This aspect of the person in African thought represents the part of the individual which is inherited through a transmission from generation to generation ... THE SHADOW Variously known as the *Swyt* (ancient Egyptian), *Ojiji* (Yoruba), *Onyinyo* (Igbo), *Lume-lume* (Bambala), *Edidingi* (Kuba), *Ye* (Fon), *Igicucu* (Banyarwanda), etc. This is an aspect of the physical body which is not just an ordinary shadow cast by sunlight.

When these different entities are organised, they form a singular entity known as a person. The element that coordinates the others is the destiny or spiritual double (which, in Kamalu's analysis, is the *Ka*). When this unity breaks down, we no longer have a balanced and centred person. The key idea is that this all has implications for the understanding and treatment of mental illness!

Dr Kamalu on pages 70 to 73 of his book suggests that mental illness may be caused by disunity among these different psychological entities. If this idea is valid, it also suggests that the practice of spirituality may be useful in certain situations for the treatment of mental ill health. This raises the possibility of putting spirituality onto a scientific context.

The English Africanist, Dr Basil Davidson, wrote the following where he noticed the connection between African traditional religions and good psychological health, unfortunately he repeats bigoted terminologies that cannot pass unchallenged in a paper of this type:

Witch-doctoring is written off in the modern world as arrant nonsense, but in traditional Africa the witch-doctor served a real and useful purpose, quite apart from his magic. He was often able to settle disputes between rivals that might have led to violence, and his knowledge of the medicinal value of herbs frequently led him to prescribe remedies that actually cured. Also, through his intimate knowledge of the lives of people in his community, and of human nature in general, it was not unusual for him to function as a sort of pre-scientific psychologist ... This faith in the healing qualities of African religion, in its physical and mental therapeutic powers helps to explain why Islam and Christianity have never completely wiped out traditional African beliefs.

CONCLUSIONS: IMPLICATIONS OF THE STUDY OF ANCIENT AND TRADITIONAL AFRICAN RELIGIONS

What are the implications for studying ancient and traditional African religions? There are parallels between the Nile Valley creation stories and traditional African creation stories. Dr Chukwunyere Kamalu on pages 103 to 143 of his book suggests that there are similarities between the creation stories of the Ancient Egyptians, the Bambara, Yoruba, Kuba, Dogon, Fon, Igbo and Songye. They tend to share similar themes of the primeval waters, transmission of the life force from the creator to all creation, four primordial elements or ancestors, chaos and order, the coming together of masculine and feminine divine powers, and the key role of the divine word or intelligence.

However, to illustrate the connection, I cite the research of Professor Finch, in a brilliant 1992 lecture, *Kmt--Customs and Culture--Continuation.* He demonstrated the connection between the Egyptian cosmology and the Dogon cosmology. I give an extract below:

> Dogon: Before the act of creation, Amma had no a place to stand. Egyptian: Prior to the creation of the Universe, Amun-Re, the creator, had no place to stand.

> Dogon: Amma brought forth an egg containing all matter in the Cosmos. Egyptian: The Egg of the World was fashioned by Ptah on a potter's wheel.

> Dogon: The Universe comes forth as a result of a thought in the mind of Amma who then uttered the creative word. Egyptian: The Neter Thoth is the mind of Amun-Re before the Universe was formed before it comes forth as an active word.

> Dogon: Amma created life on Earth from his spittle and breath. Egyptian: Atum created Tefnut from his spittle and Shu from his breath who became the ancestors of living beings.

Dogon: There are eight Nummo or primordial ancestors of man. Egyptian: There are eight primeval Neters.

Dogon: The creation of the universe begins when Amma opens his eyes. Egyptian: Light is produced from the primeval darkness when Re or Ra opens his two eyes.

Dogon: Amma created the original male female twin. Egyptian: Atum created the original male female twin, Shu and Tefnut.

There are parallels between Ancient Egyptian totemism and traditional African totemism. I begin by repeating the oft-quoted passage by Sir James Frazer, perhaps the most important authority on totemism. However, we warn the reader about the racist tone of the passage:

> If we exclude hypotheses and confine ourselves to facts, we may say broadly that totemism is practiced by many savage and barbarous peoples ... who occupy the continents and islands of the tropics and the Southern Hemisphere, together with a large part of North America, and whose complexion shades off from coal black through dark brown to red. With the doubtful exception of a few Mongoloid tribes in Assam, no yellow and no white race is totemic.

To illustrate this, on page 78 of his book *The African Origin of Civilization: Myth or Reality?,* Professor Cheikh Anta Diop noticed that the pictorial document known as *Narmer's Tablet* has "Nubian totems" depicted on it. Moreover he published images on plate 33 of his book of what he labels "Egyptian Totemic Deities." He also wrote the following on page 134: "In his book, *From Tribe to Empire,* Moret had stressed the essentially totemic character of Egyptian society."

There are parallels between Ancient Egyptian gods and traditional African gods. To illustrate this, The Rev Olumide Lucas wrote *The Religion of the Yorubas* in 1948. This controversial book claims that Yoruba religion and culture evolved in Ancient Egypt. This book has been frequently criticised by European scholars keen to deny any links between Ancient Egypt and West African culture. Nevertheless, the book began life as a University of London doctorate thesis which Dr Lucas successfully achieved. Just to put this into a context, Diop, it must be remembered, failed to achieve his doctorate from Paris the first time round where Lucas succeeded in London. Diop on page 185 quotes the following from Lucas' book:

Abundant proof of intimate connection between the ancient Egyptians and the Yoruba may be produced under this head. Most of the principle gods were well known, at one time, to the Yoruba. Among these gods are Osiris, Isis, Horus, Shu, Sut, Thoth, Khepera, Amon, Anu, Khonsu, Khnum, Khopri, Hathor, Sokaris, Ra, Seb, the four elemental deities, and others. Most of the gods survive in name or in attributes or both.

Diop, on pages 148 and 149, presents his own evidence that support some of these assertions. The main difference is that Diop has also found evidence of specifically Kushitic deities as well as Egyptian ones amongst the Yoruba:

Pédrals quotes Morié, who relates a Coptic tradition about two kings; one is unidentified, the second is King Shango, Iakouta, or Khevioso (depending on the dialect). This ruler, worshipped all over the Slave Coast (Guinea) under these different names, as the god of thunder and destruction, was, according to stories related by the Blacks, a king of Kush, whence his surname Obbato-Kouso, Shango. He passionately loved war and the hunt, and his conquests took him as far as Dahomey. The kings Biri (god of the darkness) and Aido-Khouedo (god of the rainbow) were his slaves. ["]As Morié puts it, this Obba-Kouso was born at Ife, a locality with which our author is completely unacquainted. Adorned with the title, "first-born of the Supreme God," he resulted from the incestuous love of Orougan, god of the south, and Yemadja, mother of Orougan, herself a sister of Agandjou, god of Space. Chango-Obba-Kousa's brothers are Dada, god of nature, and Ogoun, god of hunters and blacksmiths. He has three wives; Oya, Osoun, and Oba. It is quite evident that Orougan and Yemadja resemble the incestuous couple Amon (Kham) and Mout. Their son, moreover, has the surname "King of Kush." It is also evident that Osoun resembles Asoun, wife of Toubboum-Set-Typhon, later wed by Hor, son of Mesraim-Osiris, and that Dada resembles Dedan, son of Kush in one version, and of Reama in another version, with an uncertainty that the Bible aggravates even more. Finally, the Ethiopians claim that Kush also married three women, his sisters. Morié's testimony ... summarizes an essential bit of tradition common to countries coasting on the Gulf of Benin (Togo, Dahomey, Nigeria), to the Ewe, Guin, Fon, and Yoruba. The latter call their holy city Ife. (Pédrals, pp.30-31.)["] This testimony Morié had taken, as Pédrals discovered, from a booklet translated from the Arabic and published in Paris in 1666. The tradition it reveals was noted by the Copts themselves, a fact all the more important because this tradition blends with that found today in West Africa, among the populations of Dahomey, Togo, Nigeria, etc. Shango and Orougan are gods of Nigeria and the whole Gulf of Benin in general. Ife, the city whose name Morié takes from the Coptic texts without knowing that it is Nigeria's holy city, shows the close connection between Egyptian history and that of Black Africa.

Diop on page 147 cites Pédrals as saying the following: "The god Kush had altars in Memphis, Thebes, Meroë under the name of Khons, god of the sky to the Ethiopians, Hercules to the Egyptians."

This all suggests Pédrals, using information from the Copts of mediaeval Egypt, deduced that the deity Amen or Amun of the Nile Valley is Orougan in West Africa. Mut in the Nile Valley is Yemaja in West Africa. Khonsu in the Nile Valley is Shango in West Africa. Dedun of Kush is Dada in West Africa. We have already shown that some of these deities had their counterparts among the Greeks and the Romans. Khonsu is Herakles to the Greeks and Hercules to the Romans.

As we have seen Dr Chukwunyere Kamalu has demonstrated parallels between Ancient Egyptian concepts of multiple selves and traditional African concepts of multiple selves.

All of this evidence allows us to draw a powerful conclusion. The parallels in the cosmologies, totemism, gods, and conception of selves, demonstrate that a study of the Ancient Egyptian religion can elucidate traditional African religious ideas and vice versa.

It is possible that many of the readers of this essay are Christians. It may well be worth asking: Does any of this research have implications for Christianity? Key questions that may well be worth asking are:

* Is there a deification process in Christianity?

* What are the Patron Saints?

* Does Christianity have sacred rivers?

* Are the Christian adherents split into initiates and masses?

* Does the Isis, Osiris and Horus story have any bearing on Christianity?

* Does the Judgement Scene and the 42 Declarations of Innocence have any relevance to Christianity?

In closing, then, religion is one aspect of African culture. It has gone all around the world and has influenced all religious thought. It is unlikely that any later religion can separate itself completely from the early African base.

BIBLIOGRAPHY

Na'im Akbar, *Nile Valley Origins of the Science of the Mind,* in Ivan Van Sertima ed., *Egypt: Child of Africa,* US, Transaction Publishers, 1994, pp.341-354

Ifi Amadiume, *Afrikan Matriarchal Foundations,* UK, Karnak House, 1987, pp.9-10, 61-69

Yosef A. A. ben-Jochannan, *African Origins of the Major Western Religions,* US, Black Classic Press, 1970, pp.1-72

Jacob Carruthers, *Essays in Ancient Egyptian Studies,* US, Timbuktu Publishers, 1984, pp.57-67

Albert Churchward, *The Origin and Evolution of Religion,* UK, George Allen & Unwin, 1924, p.362

Basil Davidson, *African Kingdoms,* Netherlands, Time Life Books, 1967, p.128

Cheikh Anta Diop, *Civilisation or Barbarism,* US, Lawrence Hill Publishers, 1990, pp.310-313, 328-330

Cheikh Anta Diop, *The African Origin of Civilization: Myth or Reality?* US, Lawrence Hill Books, 1974, pp.78, 99, 134, 147, 148-149, 185

Charles Finch, *Ancient Kmt Deities* (Lecture), Egypt, Oberoi Hotel, 12 August 1992

Charles Finch, *Kmt--Customs and Culture--Continuation* (Lecture), Egypt, Sheraton Hotel, 8 August 1992

Charles Finch, *Echoes of the Old Darkland,* US, Khenti, 1991, pp.57-113

John G. Jackson, *Man, God, and Civilization,* US, Citadel Press, 1972, pp.57-58, 105-107, 134

John G. Jackson, *Pagan Origins of the Christ Myth,* US, American Atheist Press, 1941, whole paper

George G. M. James, *Stolen Legacy,* US, Philosophical Library, 1954, pp.139-149, 166-168

Chukwunyere Kamalu, *Person, Divinity and Nature,* UK, Karnak House, 1998, pp.53-62, 103-143

Maulana Karenga, *Introduction to Black Studies: Fourth Edition,* US, University of Sankore Press, 2010, pp.190-192

Gerald Massey, *Ancient Egypt: The Light of the World, Volumes I and II,* 1907, pp.1-45, 186-248, 727-905, 907-914

John Mbiti, *African Religions and Philosophy,* UK, Heinemann, 1990, pp.6-10, 29-97, 106

Gert Muller, *East African and Nubian Origins of the Ancient Egyptians,* UK, Pomegranate Publishing, 2013, whole book but especially pp.27-29, 35

Gert Muller, *Racial Unity of the Ancient Egyptians and Nubians,* UK, Pomegranate Publishing, 2013, whole book

Théophile Obenga, *African Philosophy: The Pharaonic Period,* Senegal, Per Ankh, 2004, pp.29-90

Innocent C. Onyewuenyi, *The African Origin of Greek Philosophy,* Nigeria, University of Nigeria Press, 1993, pp.177-219

Plutarch, *Concerning the Mysteries of Isis and Osiris,* in G. R. S. Mead, *Thrice Greatest Hermes: Volume One,* UK, John Watkins, 1906, pp.255-366

Rev Charles H. Vail, *The World's Saviours,* UK, N. L. Fowler & Co., 1913, pp.38-42, 71-72, 73, 78, 106-108, 138, 139-140

Robin Walker, *When We Ruled: Second Edition,* UK, Reklaw Education, 2013, pp.117-132, 317-345

PART TWO

THE EQUINOX AND THE REAL STORY BEHIND EASTER

INTRODUCTION: EASTER IN A GREEK ORTHODOX CHURCH

Sir James Frazer was the author of *The Golden Bough* (abridged edition, Macmillan, 1922). He was a most important authority on ancient religion. His book was originally published in 13 volumes but was later condensed into a single volume. He gave a good description of Easter ceremonies in an Orthodox Eastern church in Southern Europe. His account reads as follows (page 345):

> During the whole of Good Friday a waxen effigy of the dead Christ is exposed to view in the middle of the Greek churches and is covered with fervent kisses by the thronging crowd, while the whole church rings with melancholy, monotonous dirges. Late in the evening, when it has grown quite dark, this waxen image is carried by the priests into the street on a bier adorned with lemons, roses, jessamine, and other flowers, and there begins a grand procession of the multitude, who move in serried ranks, with slow and solemn step, through the whole town. Every man carries his taper and breaks out in doleful lamentation. At all the houses which the procession passes there are seated women with censers to fumigate the marching host. Thus the community solemnly buries its Christ as if he had just died. At last the waxen image is again deposited in the church, and the same lugubrious chants echo anew. These lamentations, accompanied by a strict fast, continue till midnight on Saturday. As the clock strikes twelve, the bishop appears and announces the glad tidings that 'Christ is risen,' to which the crowd replies, 'He is risen indeed,' and at once the whole city bursts into an uproar of joy, which finds vent in shrieks and shouts, in endless discharge of carronades and muskets, and the explosion of fire-works of every sort. In the very same hour people plunge from the extremity of the fast into the enjoyment of the Easter lamb and neat wine.

What was the Easter story as the Christians tell it?

Our key sources of the Easter story are the four accounts, known as *The Gospels.* There are, however, discrepancies in the different Gospel stories.

According to St John's Gospel, Jesus carried the cross all the way to the crucifixion. The other gospel writers wrote that Simon of Cyrene carried the cross.

St Mark wrote that Jesus underwent crucifixion at the third hour (i.e. 9 am), fifteenth of the month of Nisan. St Luke wrote that Jesus underwent crucifixion at the sixth hour (i.e. 12 noon), fifteenth of Nisan. St John wrote that Jesus had not been sentenced until after noontime but executed on fourteenth of Nisan.

What were the details?

St John recorded that Mary Magdalene was the lone visitor to the tomb. St Matthew recorded that the other Mary accompanied Mary Magdalene. St Mark recorded that Mary Magdalene and Mary the mother of James and Salome were visitors to the tomb. St Luke recorded that Mary Magdalene, Mary the mother of James, Joanna, and some other women visited the tomb.

What did they see?

According to St Matthew, the tomb was closed. According to St Luke, the large stone covering the tomb had been rolled away.

Whom did they meet?

St Matthew reported that the women met an angel. St Mark reported that they saw a young man. St Luke reported that they saw two men. St John reported that the women saw two angels.

CHAPTER ONE: ADONIS AND TAMMUZ

St Jerome was an early Christian scholar. He was responsible for the Latin Vulgate version of the Bible. He says that Bethlehem, the traditional birthplace of the Lord, was originally the seat of the sacred grove dedicated to the worship of Adonis.

Who is Adonis?

The worship of Adonis was quite popular among the Semitic speaking peoples of the Middle East around 2000 BC. Adonis was derived from a Babylonian deity called 'Tammuz'. However, Tammuz was derived from a Sumerian deity called 'Dumuzi'.

Incidentally, I read an article on the internet written by a Christian scholar who tried to DISPROVE the following ideas:

> Buddha was born on December 25th of the virgin Maya, and his birth was attended by a 'Star of Announcement,' wise men and angels singing heavenly songs.

However, in this same article was this curious passage:

> A reader has noted that Jerome in Against Jovinianus Book 1 stated that among the Gymnosophists of India, there was a tradition of Buddha being born from a virgin.

Oops! St Jerome has clearly given too much information away!

Where were the centres of Adonis worship?

The rites of Adonis were centred in Byblos in Palestine and Paphos in Cyprus. Other places were Bethlehem and Antioch. The belief system spread to the Greeks in the seventh century BC. This is how 'Tammuz' mistakenly became 'Adonis' derived from Adon (meaning 'Lord').

How was Tammuz-Adonis celebrated?

According to W. Williamson in *The Great Law* (1889, pages 53-54):

> His death was commemorated annually with mournful chants as his image lay upon a bed or bier. For three days was he bewailed as one dead, but then followed the rejoicing over his resurrection. During the ceremony of the resurrection, feasts, which took place on 25th of March, the priest, after having touched the mouths of the mourners with holy oil, murmured: "Trust ye in your Lord, for the pains which the endured have procured your salvation" … Then the people answered: "Hail to the Dove, the restorer of light."

Is this sounding familiar? Isn't this similar to Easter in a Greek Orthodox Church?

Many people reading this will be thinking: But surely this is just a coincidence?

The Rev Charles H. Vail, a church reverend, wrote *The World's Saviours,* published in London, 1913. The book is about the different deities worshipped across the world who were considered saviours of humanity. Chapter IV of this book carries the title *Death and Resurrection.*

It concerns the gods Krishna, Wittoba, Indra, Bacab, Quetzalcoatl, Prometheus, Mithra, Baccus or Dionysus, Baldur, Samheim or Bal-Sab, Tien, Aesculapius, Marsyas, Artemes, Melkarth, Sandan, Hyacinth, Marduk, Osiris, Tammuz or Adonis, Attis, Bel Merodach and Jesus.

For example, pages 86-88, has the following information on Quetzalcoatl, a deity adored by the people of ancient Mexico:

> Lord Kingsborough, the learned author of the *Antiquities of Mexico,* says, "Torquemada informs us, on the authority of Las Casas, that Quetzalcoatl had been in Yucatan, and was there adored. The interpreter of the *Vatican Codex* says of the following curious passage, that the Mexicans had a tradition that he, like Bacab, died upon the cross, and he seems to add, according to their belief, for the sins of mankind … In the fourth page of the *Borgian Ms.,* he seems to be crucified between two persons who are in the act of reviling him, who hold, as it would appear, halters in their hands, the symbol perhaps of some crime."

Surely these are just more coincidences?

CHAPTER TWO: A MYSTERY PLAY FROM ANCIENT BABYLON

The ancient Mesopotamians were the early inhabitants of Iraq (and Syria). These inhabitants included the Sumerians and the Babylonians. A considerable amount of research suggests that these peoples were largely Black in origin. Even Major-General Sir Henry Rawlinson, the founder of Mesopotamian studies, shared this view, as did his equally distinguished brother, Canon George Rawlinson - then the Canon of Canterbury.

In the British Museum, there is an ancient tablet from Babylon concerning the deity Bel. It dates back to about 2000 BC. Professor H. Zimmern discovered it in the ruins of Babylon. The deity Bel is better known by the Phoenician name 'Ba'al' Cf. Hanniba'al. The tablet concerns a 10 Act Mystery Play on the death of Bel.

In Acts One and Two, Bel is taken prisoner. Among the actors of the drama, the one representing Bel is arrested by soldiers and taken off the stage. Bel is tried in the Hall of Justice. There is a trial in the courtroom. There is a judge and witnesses who gave testimony for and against the victim. Bel is found innocent but still sentenced to death.

In Acts Three and Four, Bel is smitten. In this scene, he is abused and jeered at by the mob. Bel is led away to the mount. The actor representing Bel is taken under armed guard to a hilltop.

In Acts Five and Six, the following occurs. Act Five features Bel and two suspects. Both of the suspects are tried. One was found guilty and the other innocent. After Bel has gone to the mount, the city breaks into uproar.

In Acts Seven and Eight, Bel's clothes are carried away. The corpse of Bel is stripped of its clothing and then prepared for burial. Bel goes down into the mount and disappears from life. The body is interred in the side of the hill.

In Acts Nine and Ten, weeping women seek Bel at the tomb. Bel is brought back to life. The stone that sealed the tomb of Bel is rolled away. Bel walked out of the tomb in funeral garb. The crowd cheer until they are hoarse.

Is this sounding in any way familiar?

The Key Question is: Is this the oldest known religion of the resurrection?

CHAPTER THREE: OSIRIS AND THE EGYPTIAN
RESURRECTION

Sir E. A. Wallis Budge has the reputation of being the greatest British Egyptologist of all times. (There are, however, some Mickey-Mouse Johnny Come Lately 'Egyptologists' who run their mouths against Budge, but the truth is none of them can hold a candle to his impressive body of work).

Budge is best known for translating *The Book of the Dead* in 1913 (reprinted by University Books, US, 1960). He also wrote a two-volume work with the strange title, *Osiris: The Egyptian Religion of the Resurrection* reprinted by University Books (US, 1961). He shows that the Egyptian resurrection story is the oldest DOCUMENTED but argues that the Egyptian resurrection stories must have been derived from even older stories originating in Inner Africa.

According to Diodorus Siculus, the ancient Greek historian:

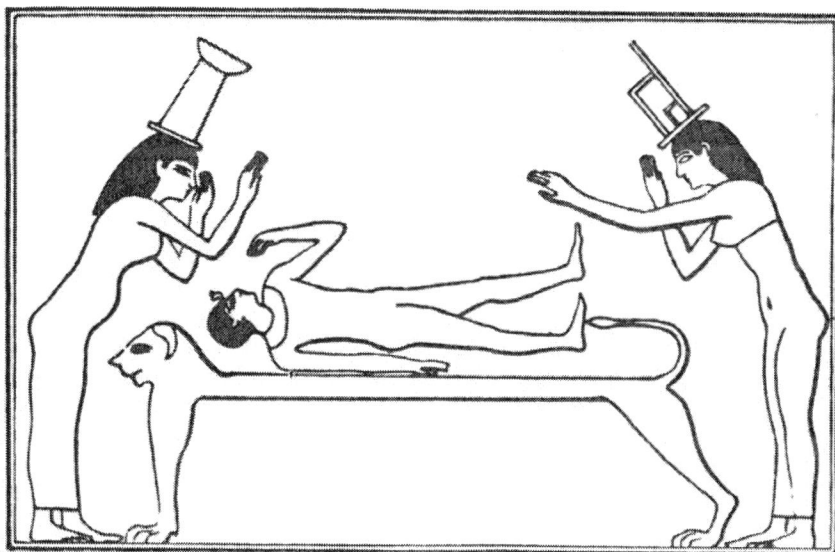

Figure 1. A bas-relief at Philae depicting Isis and Nepthys bewailing the death of Osiris.

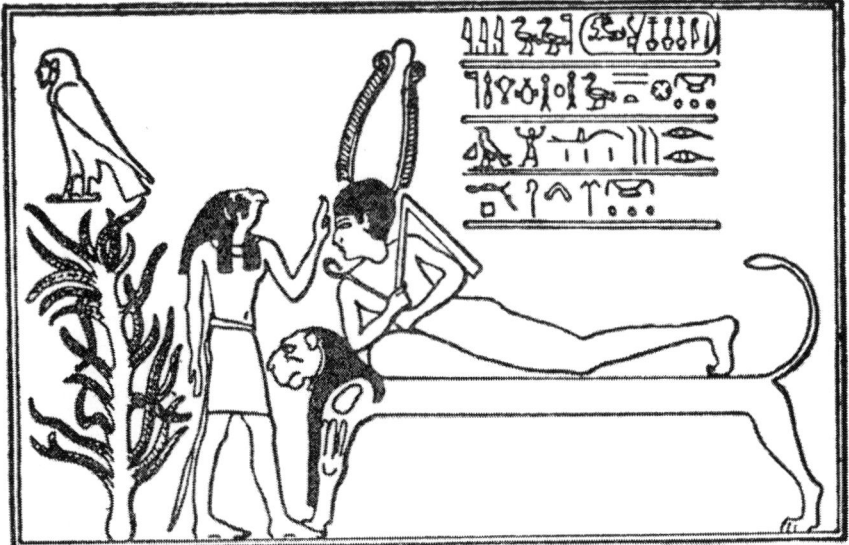

Figure 2. Osiris rising from his bier at the command of Horus.

> Now the Ethiopians, as historians relate, were the first of all men, and the
> proofs of this statement, they say, are manifest. For that they did not come into
> their land as immigrants from abroad but were the natives of it … They say also
> that the Egyptians are colonists sent out by the Ethiopians (i.e. Nubians), Osiris
> having been the leader of the colony.

Does this make Osiris originally a king or community leader in ancient
Nubia?

The ancient Roman historian Plutarch in *Concerning the Mysteries of Isis
and Osiris* best preserved the legends concerning Osiris in a treatise.
According to him, Osiris found the inhabitants of Egypt in a savage state
and conferred on them the blessings of civilisation. He encouraged the
Egyptians to cultivate grains and abandon cannibalism. He was the first is
to tread grapes to make wine.

The great king then turned over the government of Egypt to his queenly
wife Isis. He travelled around the world distributing the benefits of
civilisation to all of humanity.

After returning to Egypt, his jealous brother, Set, began to plot his
downfall. Together with 72 accomplices, Set had Osiris killed after a
banquet.

This raises a key question: Why a banquet? Is there a link between a deity
being killed after a banquet and the teachings of later religions?

Why was this story significant for the Egyptians?

According to the ancient authority Plutarch:

> Moreover, on the new moon of the month Phamenoth they [i.e. Egyptians] keep festival, calling it 'Entrance' of Osiris into the moon, as it is the beginning of spring.

The translator G. R. S. Mead added a footnote to explain "Phamenoth" that reads as follows: "roughly corr. to March."
Plutarch also says:

> And at what they call the burials of Osiris they cut the tree trunks and make it into a crescent shaped coffin, because the moon, when it approaches the sun, becomes crescent shaped and hides itself away.

This makes it clear that Osiris was a Moon deity

Did they always commemorate this at this time of the year?

During earlier times, the Ancient Egyptians celebrated the Feast of Osiris-Seker-Ptah at a different part of the year. They celebrated 10 mysteries in the month of Choiak (i.e. November 27 to December 26). The biggest of the Mysteries was the Sixth Mystery, December 22. On this festival, the Temple of Medinet Habu, for example, needed 3,694 loaves of bread, 600 cakes, 905 jugs of beer, and 33 jars of wine for the feast.

Following this was the Feast of the Erection of the Djed Pillar. This represented Osiris rising again and re-establishing stability.

The ancient Egyptian *Book of the Dead,* quoted by Albert Churchward, contains the following declaration:

> Make the word of Osiris truth against his enemies. Raise up the [Djed] which imaged the resurrection of the god, let the mummy type of the eternal be once more erected as the mainstay and divine support of all.

The *Book of the Dead* also says:

> They scent Osiris. Here is the one who is to devour me. They wait apart. The Serpent Seksek passeth over me … Osiris is he who prayeth that he may be buried. The eyes of the great one are bent down, and he doeth for thee the work of washing.

The *Book of the Dead* also says:

Thou washest thy feet in silver basins made by the skilful artificer Ptah-Seker.

What is going on here?

According to Gerald Massey, the mummified Osiris becomes the Karast. Transliterated from the hieroglyphics this becomes *krst*.

Gerald Massey, on page 870 of his book, says: "it should be borne in mind that the Ritual, as it comes to us, consists to a large extent of allusions to the matter that was made out more fully in performing the drama of the mysteries."

In other words the mummified and scented one, also known as the *krst,* is bent down, washing feet. He also prays that he may be buried quickly. He is also killed after a great banquet. Is any of this sounding familiar?

According to Professor Charles Finch, there is a link between Osiris and the hare, quoted from page 191 of his book:

> We find that all over Africa the hare is a lunar animal … the hare is also an important zootype of Osiris: as one jumps or leaps up, he is a figure of the resurrected Osiris in the act of rising up from the dead. The hare is an Egyptian ideograph which transliterates as UN, meaning 'to be' or 'being.' Osiris was known as UN-NEFER, meaning 'the good being.'

Do all continents have hares? What animal would you replace this with if you do not have hares?

CHAPTER FOUR: THE ORIGIN OF THE CONCEPT OF THE RESURRECTION

Some writers theorised that religions of the resurrection began based on the vegetation theory. For example, David Forsyth in *Psychology and Religion,* page 97, said:

> Many gods besides Christ have been supposed to die, be resurrected and ascend to heaven. This idea has now been traced back to its origin among primitive people in the annual death and resurrection of crops and plant life generally. This explains the world-wide prevalence of the notion. Among still more primitive tribes, Grant Allen showed, it is not yet understood that sown corn sprouts because of the spring sunshine, and they attribute the result of divine agency. To this end, they are accustomed at seed time to kill their tribal god - either in human or animal form - and scatter the flesh and blood over the sown fields. They believe that the seeds will not grow unless that God is sacrificed an added to them in this manner. When, therefore, the crop appears, they never doubt that it is their God coming to life again.

This theory would explain how Osiris became associated with both wheat and grapes. This may also explain the prominence of the products of wheat and grapes in religion. The main product of wheat is bread. The main product of grapes is wine. Clearly, bread and wine played important roles in the Egyptian religion as proved by the example cited above from the Temple of Medinet Habu. These products still play a role in later religions.

There is another theory that links religions to astronomy. A vast amount of scholarship from the eighteenth century to our times has endorsed this view. Among the important scholars were Charles Dupuis, Count De Volney, Gerald Massey, Albert Churchward and Professor Charles Finch.

We have already seen that Osiris was associated with the moon. At the end of the lunar cycle, the moon disappears for two nights and reappears on the third. It is also important to note that all religions are divided into initiates and masses. Their levels of understanding would be vastly different.

According to the findings of Dupuis and De Volney, the early Africans were systematically stargazing at least 15,000 years ago. They were the

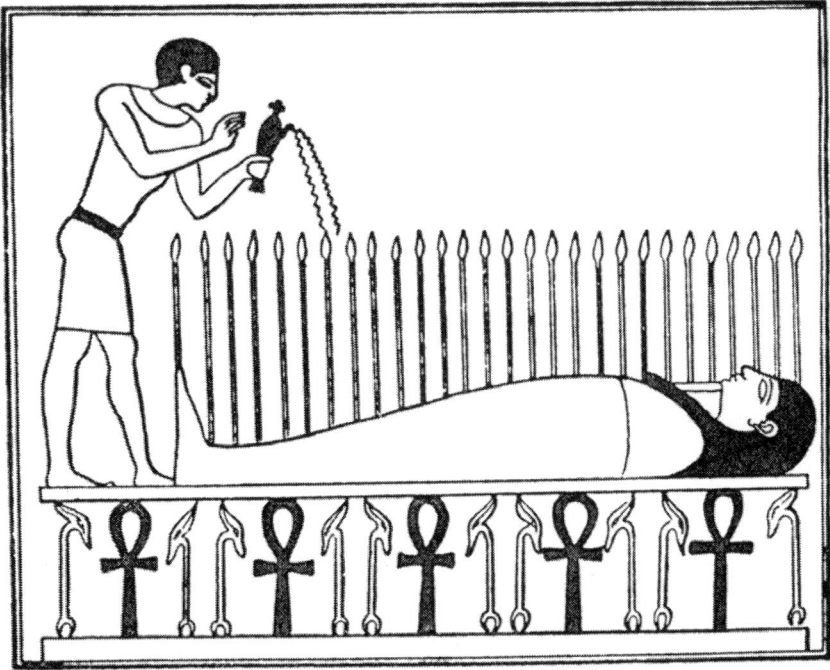

Figure 3. A bas-relief from Philae depicting Osiris-Nepri with wheat growing out of his body.

first to divide the heavens into 12 houses. These houses became signs of the zodiac and also months of the year.

In the course of a year, it appears from Earth that the Sun has travelled through the 12 signs of the zodiac. During the year, nights are longer than days in winter and days are longer than nights in summer. On March 21, days and nights are of equal length, this is the Vernal Equinox.

In the words of Count De Volney in *The Ruins or Meditations on the Revolutions of Empires and the Law of Nature* (US, 1802, page 121):

> It was, then, on the borders of the upper Nile, among a black race of men, that was organised the complicated system of the worship of the stars, considered in relation to the productions of the earth and the labours of agriculture; and this first worship, characterized by their adoration under their own forms and natural attributes, was a simple proceeding of the human mind.

So what?

All religions that understood this made the number 12 sacred. The Greeks

Figure 4. Osiris sitting under a bunch of grapes.

and Romans had the 12 Labours of Herakles or Hercules. The Sumerians had the 12 Tablets of Gilgamesh. One Egyptian papyrus, the *Papyrus of Ani,* has 12 deities in judgement in Amenta presiding over the souls of the dead (Other papyri give different numbers).

How does it work?

December 22 is the shortest day of the year. December 25 is significantly longer than the previous days. Ancient religions celebrated this as the birth of the new Sun.

On March 21, days and nights are of equal length. This is the point at which the sun passes over the celestial equator. This is the true origin of the term 'Passover'. After this date, the sun conquers darkness, because days are increasingly longer than nights.

When is Easter?

The Church calculates Easter as the first full moon after the Vernal Equinox. The Christians then celebrate the Friday and Sunday that follows this. During the time of Pope St Victor I (189-199 AD), Easter was formally celebrated across the whole Roman Church on the Sunday. Incidentally, this Pope was one of three great individuals who are thought to have been of African stock.

Who among you reading this can do this calculation for Easter next year?

Does this not make it CLEAR the difference between what the initiates know, and what the masses know?

The Christian Church has always had initiates among its ranks who could do these calculations.

CONCLUSION: A FRESH PERSPECTIVE ON EASTER

The Vernal Equinox has always been a sacred time. Religions of death and resurrection have existed all over the globe. Even specifics such as the deity being aware of being betrayed, praying that they may be buried quickly, being tried, executed on a mount, wailing women, criminals, etcetera, have been around for a long time. The deity being associated with the products of wheat and the products of grapes have been around for a long time. The cross, the hare (now the Easter Bunny), the banquet, and the washing of feet have been around for a long time. Finally, the split between what the masses are told about the belief system and what the initiates are told has been consistent across all religions.

Let me give the final word to the Reverend Charles H. Vail. In the *Conclusion* of his book *The World's Saviours,* he says the following (pages 193-195):

> The foregoing study of the World's Saviours shows clearly the unity of religions. The similarities in the lives, teachings, symbols, ceremonies, etc., evidence a common origin … The great Saviours have always brought the same message to the world. The religions founded by them possess practically the same doctrines, symbols, rites, precepts, while the differences are merely non-essentials.

BIBLIOGRAPHY

Ishakamusa Barashango, *Afrikan Genesis,* US, Fourth Dynasty, 1991

Yosef ben-Jochannan, *African Origins of the Major Western Religions,* US, BCP, 1970

Sir E. A. Wallis Budge, *Osiris: The Egyptian Religion of the Resurrection,* 2-Volumes, reprinted by University Books, US, 1961

Albert Churchward, *The Origin and Evolution of Religion,* London, 1924

Count De Volney, *The Ruins or Meditations on the Revolutions of Empires and the Law of Nature,* US, 1802

Charles S. Finch, *Echoes of the Old Darkland,* US, Khenti, 1991

David Forsyth, *Psychology and Religion,* London, 1935

Sir James Frazer, *The Golden Bough, abridged edition,* Macmillan, 1922

John G. Jackson, *Christianity Before Christ,* US, AA Press, 1985 edition ONLY

Gerald Massey, *Ancient Egypt: Light of the World, Volume 2,* London, 1907

Rev Charles H. Vail, *The World's Saviours,* London, 1913

PART THREE

UNDERSTANDING THE BOOK OF THE DEAD

It was undoubtedly Kushites who rendered possible the Aryan advance, and who played the part of a civilizing Rome thousands of years before Roma's birth. It was their vast mythology and strange legends that passed as Lord Bacon wrote "like light air into the flutes of Grecians, there to be modulated as best suited Grecian fancies." Indeed, it is manifest from many old writings, that it was their tales, myths, traditions and histories that lay at base of the Western World's thought and legendary lore. These so impressed all subsequent races and entered so deeply and minutely into all Aryan mythologies that many writers now think Aryans can only claim to have added to the superstructure and complexion of Ethiopian myths and mythical history.

- Major General J. G. R. Forlong, 1883

INTRODUCTION

Years ago, I first came across mention of the *Book of the Dead,* particularly the *Papyrus of Ani* version, in a book by our dearly beloved elder scholar Professor Yosef ben-Jochannan. The Professor made the following extravagant claim:

> The Gods or Orishas of the Yoruba religion of West Africa, headed by the Supreme Being - OLUDUMARE, aided by His ancestral spirits; and of course VODUM - the Supreme Being or God of the Voodoo religion; also teach the same 'TRUTH' as do the gods - Jehovah of the Hebrews, Jesus Christ of Nazareth of the Christians, and Al'lah of the Muslims religion. Yet 'metaphysics' and 'philosophy' have been taught in a manner suggestive of their non-existence in the two African religions of West Africa mentioned above [i.e. Yoruba and Voodoo], but not of the other three they have labelled 'Western Religions' forgetting that the fundamental base of all three [i.e. Judaism, Christianity and Islam] originated at the same source the other two also took root; such, however, being typical of professors who are oriented to the type of Anglo-Saxon Protestant Judaeo-Christian Greek-centric racism and religious bigotry that permeated 'Western' education. Nevertheless they cannot escape history; the BOOK OF THE DEAD, PAPYRUS OF ANI, NEGATIVE CONFESSIONS, and other major works by the ancient indigenous Africans constantly remain as the ghosts that haunt them.

When I first read that, my reaction was 'Wow!' I bought the *Papyrus of Ani,* tried to read it, and was thoroughly dismayed! I thought the book was African 'mumbo-jumbo'.

This was still my view until I saw the British Museum pre-exhibition on 31 October 2010 *Journey into the Afterlife* and the excellent catalogue edited by Professor John Taylor.

I have since changed my mind. Professor ben-Jochannan was ABSOLUTELY CORRECT!

The *Book of the Dead* itself was a roll of papyrus. A typical roll varied from 1 m to 40 m in length, and from 15 to 45 cm in width. On the backs of these rolls was the title, Peret Em Heru i.e. book of the 'coming forth by day'. The names and titles of the owner were often written in a different hand to the scribe who wrote or copied the body of the text. This suggests that the rolls were produced in workshops awaiting orders. These texts

Figure 1. Setting up the Djed from a bas-relief at Abydos.

were probably kept in some archival, library or storage system before being purchased. The most famous *Peret Em Heru* roll of them all was the one purchased by Ani, which is why it is called the *Papyrus of Ani.*

Chapter 18 of the text has a powerful statement quoted by Dr Albert Churchward that summed up he ethos of the belief systam:

> Make the word of Osiris truth against his enemies. Raise up the [Djed] which image the resurrection of the god, let the mummy type of the eternal be once more erected as the mainstay and divine support of all.

CHAPTER ONE: EGYPTIAN IDEAS AND CONCEPTS OF LIFE AND DEATH

The Egyptians saw life as a series of transformations: birth, growing up, parenthood, old age, death, followed by rebirth. This cyclical view of life echoed the recurring patterns of natural phenomena, such as the motions of the heavenly bodies, the annual flooding of the Nile, or the growth of crops. These cycles continued forever leading to the view that beyond the threshold of death, human existence would also go on forever.

Death, however, was seen as the disintegration of the person, isolation from one's social context, an enemy to be fought against, and a sequence in transformation representing a new phase of being.

Human existence as part of nature was codified in myth. Our dearly beloved scholar Professor Charles Finch explains myth as 'a symbolic or typological means of representing the psychic, cultural, and natural dimensions of reality.'

The supernatural and natural worlds were thought to be closely connected. For example, the Pharaoh, on behalf of his subjects, made offerings to the deities to sustain and satisfy them. In turn, the deities gave life to human beings. Illustrating this is an inscription from one of the tombs that reads: 'An offering which the King gives to Osiris ... so that he might give bread, beer, meat, and fowl to the spirit of the deceased.'

There was a boundary between the world of the living and the world of the dead. The Pharaoh was seen as an intermediary between both worlds. Magic and ritual were also seen as ways of crossing from the world of the living to the world of the deities and the dead.

The ancient Egyptians saw a person as a composite of different aspects and modes of existence called *kheperu*. There was the physical body. There was the heart, which was probably considered the most important (i.e. the *ab*). There was the name. There was the shadow. There were also spirit aspects called the *ka* and the *ba*.

The *ka* was the life force and was passed on from parent to child through generations. It was also personal to each individual as a kind of double. It was often represented in art as an exact copy of the individual. After death

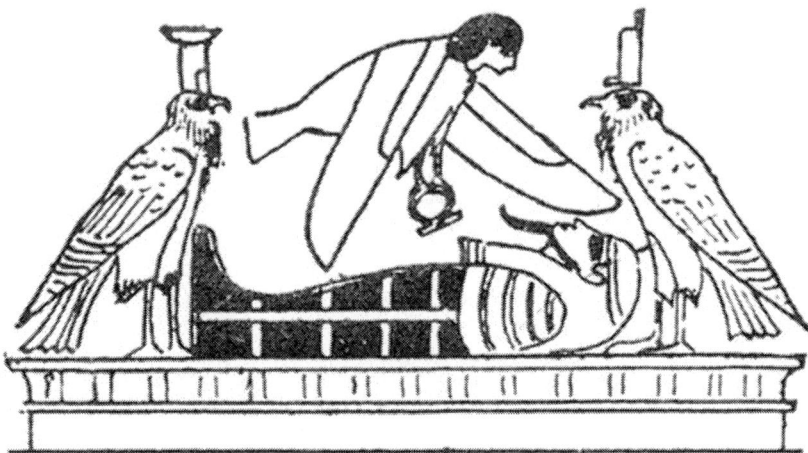

Figure 2. The *ba* hovering over the mummy of the deceased.

it remained at the tomb and was nourished by food offerings from the living.

The *ba* was the soul. It represented the personality of the individual and remained with them during life. After death it acquired the ability to move freely and independently of the body. It was depicted as a human headed bird. It could leave the mummified body by day and would be reunited with it each night.

Scholars, however, do not agree on the translations and meanings of the Ancient Egyptian elements that make up a human being. Sir E. A. Wallis Budge, the great English Egyptologist of the early 1900s, thinks that there was a *khat* physical body, *sah* spiritual body, *ba* soul, *ka* double, *khu* (nowadays scholars think this should be written as *akh*) spiritual intelligence as a celestial being, *ab* heart, *sekhem* power or vital force, *khaibit* shadow and *ren* name.

Chukwunyere Kamalu, a Nigerian philosopher based in London, in *Person, Divinity and Nature* (UK, Karnak House, 1998) presents his own theories and shows that many other African cultures have similar and related concepts to those of the ancient Egyptians.

What happens to an individual at death?

Once dead, these aspects of the self became divided. They can only be united again after the correct rituals and spells had been undergone.

Mummification transformed the dead physically. The ritual and magical processes transformed the dead spiritually. They became an *akh* (a transfigured spirit) or an *akhu* (the blessed dead i.e. plural). The corpse would be preserved, placed in a tomb, and its *ka* was supplied with food and supplies. Once transformed into an *akh*, the dead would be assimilated to specific deities connected with creation and rebirth.

Who were these specific deities?

One of these was Ra. He was associated with the sun and travelled across the sky bringing life to the inhabitants of earth. At sunset he symbolically died and journeyed through the Netherworld to re-emerge in the east at dawn representing rebirth. The Egyptians believed they might partake in this endless cycle of recurring life. Their literature gives praise to Ra to gain admittance with him.

Another deity was Osiris. He ruled as king but was treacherously murdered by Set who took his place. Isis had him mummified and resurrected to life. His son, Horus, battled Set to avenge Osiris. Osiris became the eternal ruler in the realm of the dead. The Egyptians believed that they may have their life renewed just as Osiris had. It even became standard to write the name 'Osiris' before the name of the deceased who now became 'the Osiris of X'.

Eventually the two stories, of Ra and Osiris, became one where Ra travels across the sky and disappears into the netherworld where he embraces and merges with Osiris. For example, the *Book of the Dead*, Chapter 17, says:

> I know yesterday. I know tomorrow. 'What does this mean?' 'Yesterday' is Osiris. 'Tomorrow' is Ra.

Thus Ra became the *ba* of Osiris. Similarly, other stories connected Ra, Horus, Atum and Amen into one concept. We can continue to generalise in this way linking ALL the different divine images and concepts into one thing i.e. monotheism. Sir E. A. Wallis Budge wrote:

> It is quite true that the Egyptians paid honour to a number of gods, a number so large that the list of their names would fill a volume, but it is equally true that the educated classes in Egypt at all times never placed the "gods" on the same level as God, and they never imagined that their views on this point could be mistaken.

However, my mentor Dr Femi Biko compares the polytheistic and monotheistic god concept to water. There is 'water,' not 'one' water or 'many' waters just 'water'. Similarly, there aren't 'many gods' or 'one god,' but 'God.'

What did Osiris mean to the dead person?

Mummification transformed the dead body into an eternal image called a *sah*. The *sah* form and pose assimilated the deceased to Osiris. The bandages were tied tightly to preserve the corpse and to restrict movement. The *Pyramid Texts* speak of the Pharaoh being urged to loosen and throw off the confining bandages. The dead were often shown as bas, men and women enjoying full use of their bodies.

What does this tell us about the Egyptian belief system?

Professor John Taylor of the British Museum, whom I shall frequently cite, made the following curious claim:

> This does not of course mean that the body was expected to arise physically from its coffin and walk.

Elsewhere he reiterates this dubious claim:

> As early as the Old Kingdom, passages in the *Pyramid Texts* assure the dead king that he will loosen his bandages and throw them off. They did not of course envisage a literal resurrection of the corpse, but the figurative release from the bonds of death. In keeping with this concept, the dead enjoying the afterlife are depicted not as mummies but as people in daily dress and having full command of their faculties.

I ask the question: If that is not what it means, then what does it mean? I believe that the Professor is attempting to package the Egyptian belief system in ways not to offend Christians. But truth is truth. Here we have clear evidence that the Egyptians believed in the concept of the resurrection of the dead.

What was the ultimate aim of the righteous dead?

In early times, the Egyptians presented the realm of the dead as the West, where the sun sets. This can only have been symbolic because the realm of the dead could not be accessed from the physical world except from the location of tombs. During the Old Kingdom period, the Pharaoh ascended from his pyramid to the sky. He dwelt among the circumpolar stars and later the boat of Ra. However, commoners dwelt with Osiris in the Netherworld.

In later periods the common idea was that the *ba* or *akh* could revisit the world of the living, travel with Ra, or enter Duat i.e. the realm of Osiris.

One category of the dead were known as the *mutu* (i.e. the damned) including the unrighteous dead and people executed as enemies. Some spells used by living people warded off bad dreams and illnesses thought to have been caused by the *mutu*.

Another category of the dead was the *akh* (i.e. the blessed). They were venerated as ancestors at the home in the form of sculpted busts or stelae, a practice seen in other African societies. The living still had to keep the *akhu* on side by ensuring that their tombs were in good order and the offerings were kept up. One highly valued item that the living should provide for the dead was the *Book of the Dead*.

Dr Femi Biko called traditional African religions 'Ancestralism.' Professor John Taylor states:

> One of the most striking differences between ancient Egyptian religion and modern monotheistic religions is in their attitudes toward the dead: according to the modern view, contact with the dead is usually regarded as taboo; to the ancient Egyptians it was an accepted part of the world. Family ties remained active: indeed, a man depended on his relatives to arrange his burial and to support his spirit via the mortuary cult, visiting the tomb periodically to make offerings. The nature of the treatment of the dead by the living could have serious consequences, for the dead could both help the living and cause them harm.

Notice the Christian bias in the presentation of the data i.e. 'cult'. However, notice also the similarity between these belief systems and those prevailing elsewhere among African peoples. We will see other examples of similarity elsewhere in this essay.

Living people even wrote letters to the dead asking for help with sickness, persecution or other troubles. Those letters were typically of five parts. They would begin with an address to the dead person. There would be greetings to the deceased. Following this would be praise for the deceased encourage them to help the living. After this would be a description of the problem. Finally, there would be an appeal to the deceased to intervene and help the living.

A key Egyptian concept was *heka,* which is of controversial meanings. Professor Taylor says it means 'magic'.

According to him, the deities possessed *heka.* This power was also accessible to priests, ordinary people, and ancestors, if they knew how to access it. *Heka* could be used to combat the challenges posed by childbirth, sickness and snakebites. It could also be used by the dead in their challenges in the afterlife.

Others scholars think the term means 'power'. However, David Rankine, an authority on the practice of magic, says:

> It is impossible to practice Egyptian magic without incorporating the symbols and worship of the gods.

Therefore one key discussion the Black Community needs to have is: What are the similarities and differences between prayers, spells, 'science' and magic?

There were two types of *heka* infused texts: The mortuary liturgies and recitations on the one hand, and the *Book of the Dead* on the other.

The mortuary liturgies and recitations were the actual words of rituals performed by the living for the benefit of the dead while they were being mummified or buried.

The *Book of the Dead* contains a large range of *heka* infused texts including prayers and hymns to the deities, spells or utterances to repel enemies and give protection, spells or utterances to empower the individual with divine powers, spells or utterances to demonstrate knowledge, and spells or utterances to allow the individual to pass in safety.

Written and spoken words were believed to have power in themselves. For example, the Egyptians called their script 'medu neter' (i.e. word of God). The Greeks called the script 'hieroglyphics' (i.e. sacred writings). It is interesting to compare these ideas with those of later religions. Moreover, pronouncing the name of something was thought to bring it into existence as when Ptah conceived of things in his mind and then brought them into existence by uttering their names. It interesting to compare this idea with those in later African cultures.

I ask: Is this why during enslavement Europeans and Arabs suppressed our names? Moreover: Is this why in modern African cultures people only reveal part of their names to others?

As an example, in the *Book of the Dead* when the individual encounters negative forces he or she should say 'I know you and I know your names' before commanding the negative elements to depart.

Another way in which the texts give power is for the dead speaker to identify themselves with being an actual deity, particularly Osiris, Horus, Ra or Atum. As an example, Chapter 43 says:

> I am put together, just and young, for I indeed am Osiris, the Lord of Eternity.

The idea of providing the dead with texts that provided them with *heka* began with the *Pyramid Texts,* then the *Coffin Texts.* These ideas evolved into the *Book of the Dead.*

CHAPTER TWO: USING THE *BOOK OF THE DEAD*

In the *Book of the Dead,* the chapters have headings in red ink, the body text is in black ink and sometimes special words are emphasised in red or white ink. Red ink was also used to give the correct ritual instructions on how to use and recite the utterances. When written on walls or coffins, the utterances were written in blue.

The language used for the utterances was Middle Egyptian. Since the *Book of the Dead* was a Second Intermediate Period to New Kingdom text, using Middle Egyptian gave the book an archaic feel. It is interesting to compare this with similar practices in later religions.

For the utterances to work, there were instructions which specified the appropriate time of day for the actions to be carried out. For example Chapter 144 states:

> To be recited and erased, item by item, after reciting these directions, four hours
> of the day having passed, and taking great care as to the position [of the sun] in
> the sky.

Sometimes the spells involve the transfer of power to a particular object such as an amulet or a model animal. At a word of command, these animals were supposed to come to life.

What use were these utterances, spells or prayers in everyday life?

Chapter 17 says:

> If a man speaks this spell when he is in a state of purity, it means going forth
> after death into the day and assuming whatever shape he desires. As for anyone
> who shall read it daily for his own benefit, it means being hale on earth; he shall
> come forth from every fire and nothing evil shall reach him.

Chapter 71 says:

> As for him who shall recite this spell, it means prosperity on earth with Ra and
> a goodly burial with Osiris.

What is in the *Book of the Dead?*

A typical *Book of the Dead* may contain the following content. There would be an introductory adoration scene. Chapter 1 spoke of the dead person's arrival in the Netherworld. Chapter 17 has the dead person identifying with the deity Atum. There were chapters for the dead person to secure essential abilities necessary to negotiate the Netherworld.

There were also chapters referring to the heart, chapters calling for protection against dangerous animals, chapters for providing air and water in the necropolis for the benefit of the dead person, and chapters that allow the dead person to transform into a *ba,* the deity Ptah, a crocodile, a snake, or a lotus, which incidentally was a symbol of rebirth.

Chapter 89 concerns the *ba* regularly reuniting with the corpse at night. There were chapters that concerned the ferryboat, which is a reference to the journey through the Netherworld where the deceased had to show knowledge of the parts of ships. Some chapters concerned the journey of the dead in the boat of Ra. Other chapters concerned the gates and their daemon like guardians. There were chapters that concerned knowledge of mysterious regions such as the 14 mounds of the Netherworld.

Chapter 125 is the judgement scene before Osiris. The British Museum claim:

> This spell seems to form the core of each roll.

This suggests Chapter 125 was the centrepiece of the entire Egyptian belief system.

CHAPTER THREE: THE PREHISTORY OF THE *BOOK OF THE DEAD*

What is the origin of the Book of the Dead?

The *Book of the Dead* was claimed to be of divine origins. Gerald Massey, author of the classic *Ancient Egypt: The Light of the World*, quotes the following:

> Here I am glorified and filled with soul and power, and provided with the writings of [Thoth].

Another problem concerns the question: Are we defining the *Book of the Dead* simply as a papyrus roll or are we tracing its ideas back to the point of origin?

It is claimed on behalf of Chapter 30B that:

> This spell was found in Hermopolis, under the feet of this god. It was written on a block of mineral of Upper Egypt in the writing of the god himself, and was discovered in the time of ... Menkaure. It was the king's son ... who found it while he was going around making an inspection of the temples.

Consequently, some scholars date the *Book of the Dead* to times exceedingly remote i.e. to the time of the deity Thoth. Others date the text to the Egyptian Fourth Dynasty i.e. the time of Pharaoh Menkaure. However, Professor Taylor seems to define the *Book of the Dead* as new material definitely not contained in the *Pyramid Texts* or the *Coffin Texts*. He therefore dates its origin to the Egyptian Dynasty XIII.

The *Pyramid Texts* date back to the time of Pharaoh Unas of Dynasty V. The text concerns the Pharaoh's survival into the afterlife. The Netherworld was thought to be located in the sky and ruled by Ra. The texts contained hymns, prayers, liturgies and magical utterances.

By the time of Dynasty VI, these funerary texts were made available to Queens.

Towards the end of the Old Kingdom period, local governors and high-ranking officials decorated their tombs and coffins with these funerary texts. They began to identify themselves with Osiris, the deity of the Netherworld, who gave hope to the dead by his example of resurrection.

The next development was the *Coffin Texts*. They were written on the inner surfaces of wooden coffins, on tomb walls, and on papyri. Some of their chapters were based on the *Pyramid Texts* but now used modernised grammar. The *Coffin Texts* now had headings and some included illustrations.

The *Book of the Dead* was composed in the city of Waset. These texts began to be written at the beginning of the Second Intermediate Period. There were nearly 200 chapters which comprise this collection, some of which were based on the old *Coffin Texts* but with new additions. The oldest known occurrence of the *Book of the Dead* was found on the coffin of Queen Mentuhotep of Dynasty XIII.

By the New Kingdom period, the Egyptians replaced wooden coffins with anthropoid coffins leaving little room to write the *Book of the Dead* chapters. Consequently, the texts were written on shrouds and papyrus rolls instead. By the time of Dynasty XVIII the text had fully developed, but there was no agreed canon, order, or number of utterances. Consequently each papyrus roll was unique - we shall discuss why this is the case later on.

No *Book of the Dead* rolls have survived dating from the Akhenaten period. This is possibly because of the undermining of the traditional belief system during his time.

In later times, other funerary texts were used as well as the *Book of the Dead*. Among these were the *Amduat*, the *Documents of Breathing* and *The Book of Traversing Eternity*.

CHAPTER FOUR: PREPARATION FOR THE DUAT

On the day of burial, according to the ancient Greek historian Herodotus:

> In the case of people in whose houses there perishes a man of some consequence, all the females from these houses smear their heads with dust, and sometimes also the face, and then they leave the corpse in the house and themselves wander through the town beat their breasts, with garments girt up revealing their breasts, and with them all his female relatives. And the males beat their breasts separately, these too with their garments girt up. When they have done this, so do they carry forth the corpse to be mummified.

The corpse was taken from the house to a place where it would be embalmed. It was the tradition to mummify individuals on the west side of the Nile where the embalmers workshops were located. Incantations were spoken as the body was embalmed but none of these words appear in the *Book of the Dead* although something similar does appear in Chapter 154. Chapter 154 explains the importance of mummification:

> Hail to you, my father Osiris! You shall possess your body; you shall not become corrupt, you shall not have worms, you shall not be distended, you shall not stink, you shall not become putrid, you shall not become worms.

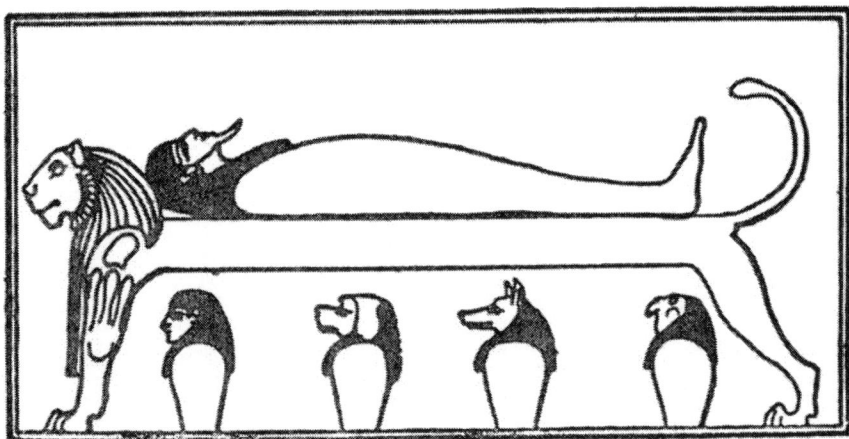

Figure 3. Osiris on his bier with the 4 canopic jars.

Figure 4. Sunrise from the *Papyrus of Hunefer* showing the Djed as the backbone of Osiris.

During mummification, the most perishable organs were removed. The body itself was dried using natron and was anointed with oils and resins. Incense was also used. The cavities were packed and the corpse was wrapped in layers of linen in the *sah* form, to emphasise purity and divinity. The enveloping of the body signified the gestation process from which the dead would eventually emerge reborn. In some situations, the internal organs were placed in four canopic jars.

After this, the mummy was given amulets and a mask, i.e. 'the head of mystery.' Gold and lapis lazuli represented the skin and the hair of the divine ones. In fact, the whole body became associated with a corresponding deity. To cite Chapter 42:

> My hair is Nun; my face is Ra; my eyes are Hathor; my ears are Wepwawet; my nose is She who presides over her lotus leaf; my lips are Anubis; my molars are Selkis; my incisors are Isis the goddess; my arms is the Ram, the Lord of Mendes ...

Among the amulets given to protect the mummy were the djed, the Isis knot, the heart scarab, the heart, the headrest, and the papyrus column.

The djed was originally associated with Sokar and represented stability. Its symbolism was later associated with Osiris where it became his backbone. The re-erection of the Djed was the central public ritual in the Egyptian religion.

Deities were also thought to stand around and protect the mummy at night from negative forces.

An Egyptian story, the *Tale of Sinuhe,* describes what happened next, i.e. the burial ritual:

> Think of the day of burial, the passage to the state of reverence, when a night is assigned to you of ointments and wrappings from the hands of Tayit and the funeral procession is made for you on the day of burial, the mummy case being of gold, its head of lapis lazuli, and a canopy being over you as you lie in the hearse, Oxon drawing you and musicians being before you, and the dance of the muu is performed at the door of your tomb, and the offering list is read for you, and sacrifices made at your offering stone.

What happened next?

The mummy was held upright by Anubis (i.e. a priest dressed as Anubis) in front of a stela, and literally stood before Ra i.e. the sun.

This was followed by the Opening of the Mouth, a ritual which symbolically allowed the mummy to regain the use of his mouth, eyes, ears and nose - all necessary in the afterlife. For example, Chapter 22 says:

> My mouth has been given to me that I may speak with it in the presence of the Great God.

This ritual involved a leopard-skinned priest touching the face mask with an adze, a chisel, and a ram's headed rod.

The second part of the ritual involved the sacrifice of calf, cutting off its foreleg and removing its heart while still alive. The live foreleg and heart were presented to the mummy, which symbolised the transfer of life. The Opening of the Mouth uses all the symbolism of the birth of a child, so in this case it represents rebirth. Finally, at some point in the ritual, hymns and prayers would be directed to the deities Osiris and Ra.

Following this, the mummy was placed in the tomb. The Egyptians called this 'the day of joining the earth.' Also placed in the tomb were the other burial goods and the canopic jars.

Figure 5. The mummy standing before Ra held up by Anubis.

A tomb usually had the burial chamber deep into the ground and inaccessible. It also had a chapel where relatives could make offerings. The tomb was symbolic of the womb of Nut and thus represented rebirth. Nut is the goddess who swallows the sun each night. She gives birth to the sun each morning.

The mummy remained inaccessible in the tomb. The *ka* would venture from the tomb to the chapel to receive the offerings from the living as real or symbolic foodstuffs. The living would bring offerings to the chapel and say prayers that mentions the person's name. Pronouncing the name perpetuated the dead person's existence. Illustrating this, Chapter 25 says:

> I have put my name in the Upper Egyptian shrine, I [have] made my name to
> be remembered in the lower Egyptian shrine.

Again, it is interesting to compare these practices with those practised elsewhere in Africa.

The *ba* would be able to 'come forth by day' unrestricted by the limitations of the tomb but would rejoin the mummy at night. The *ba* could revisit the world of the living, journey with Ra, or travel to the dominions of Osiris. The rejoining of the mummy at night rejuvenated it just as Osiris and Ra rejuvenated each other. But the body must remain intact and cannot be corrupted.

Figure 6. Scene from Chapter 151. The mummy is in the middle being embalmed by Anubis. Isis and Nepthys kneel at either end of the bed. Two of the amulets are visible: the djed and the jackal.

As well as corruption, the body had to be protected from the forces of Set, wild animals, and grave robbers. Set had dismembered Osiris' body and scattered the pieces across Egypt. No individual wanted this to happen to them.

Who guarded the body?

Chapter 151 has a detailed image which shows the following. The mummy is in the middle. The *ba* is nearby. Anubis is shown embalming the corpse. By the way, Gerald Massey insists that the mummified and anointed corpse became the *karas* or *karast* cf. Christ. Isis and Nepthys kneel at either end of the bed. On each of the four walls are amulets--a mummified individual, a djed, a jackal, and a torch. They also symbolise the four cardinal points. At the four corners were the four 'sons of Horus'--Imsety, Hapy, Duamutef and Qebehseneuf. They guard the corpse.

CHAPTER FIVE: IN THE DUAT OR THE MYSTERIES OF AMENTA

The dead were now in the realm of the Duat. This can be seen as the Netherworld, the Underworld or even inside the body of Nut like the sun at night. According to Professor Taylor, it was depicted in art with land, fields, rivers, lakes, pathways, caverns and living creatures, emphasising the Egyptian landscape that they knew. It also contained turquoise trees, iron walls, and lakes of fire, emphasising elements of strangeness. There were also buildings with gates and openings.

However, Gert Muller in *East African and Nubian Origins of the Ancient Egyptians* suggests that the strange images in the Duat are actually references to real places in Central East Africa.

Pyramid Text 473, for instance, mentions 'the field of malachite'. *Pyramid Text 1784* mentions 'the lakes of malachite.' There is a Dynasty V fragmentary autobiographical text that says 'The Malachite Country ... Punt 80,000 measures of myrrh.' Another *Pyramid Text* has the phrase 'Horus, lord of malachite.' Since Punt was in the Horn of Africa, this suggests the malachite field and lakes were in or near this region. Moreover Horus was considered the lord over this region.

Chapter 17 in the *Book of the Dead* says:

> 'Chaos-god' is the name of one; 'Sea' is the name of the other. They are the Lake of Natron and the Lake of Maat ... As for that Great God who is in them, he is Re himself.

Tanzania has a volcano whose name in Maasai means 'Mountain of God.' Next to it is a place that is even today called Lake Natron. This is a soda lake that some believe was once connected to a twin. Muller quotes Michael Wood as saying: 'a curious layer of algae made Lake Natron look as if it had been left over from the time when the earth was molten lava and fire.' Its partner may have been Magadi in Kenya. Thus the Lake of Fire may well have been the volcano erupting molten lava into or near the Lake of Natron. The Lake of Maat could well have been Magadi. Moreover Ra was associated with these lakes. In addition, the mountain in this region is even today called the Mountain of God by at least one of the peoples in the region.

Chapter 108 of the *Book of the Dead* says:

> As for the mountain of Bakhu on which the sky rests ... Sobk, Lord of Bakhu, is in the east of that mountain; his temple is of cornelian.

This mountain may well have been Mount Kenya and is now sacred to the Kikuyu. The tallest mountain in Kenya and the second highest in Africa, it could certainly be described as a mountain 'on which the sky rests.' Moreover, this suggests that Sobek, a deity imagined as a crocodile, was considered to have come from this region.

Muller argues that the *Book of Gates,* another Egyptian text, provides additional information about the strange imagery in the Duat. There is a passage in the text that says:

> [Here is] the lake of water which is in the Tuat, and is surrounded by the gods who are arrayed in their apparel ... The water of this lake is boiling hot, and the birds betake themselves to flight when they see the waters thereof, and when they smell the foetid smell which is in it.

Lake Natron is known to reach surface temperatures regularly above 60C. In addition, the lake periodically becomes so alkaline that it approaches pure ammonia. Despite this, however, in 1954 an ornithologist called Leslie Brown discovered there the largest breeding colony of Lesser Flamingoes in the world. These birds had Lake Natron as their home! Brown himself described the lake as 'evil, fetid, foul ... stinking and vile.' However, the alkalinity of the lake can periodically turn deadly to these flamingos depending on the rainfall. It is at this point that the flamingos would betake themselves to flight.

The sacred texts mention the sycamore tree. Sacred to Hathor, biologists claim it was originally distributed between South Africa up to Sudan and Ethiopia (also Yemen). This suggests that it only came into Egypt by human intervention.

The texts also mention a 51 feet serpent. Muller argues that the closest living reality to this is the African Rock Python at 28 feet. It originally had a distribution just like the sycamore tree. Other animals mentioned in the texts are waterfowl, geese, pelicans and herons. All of these are well represented in the biodiversity of Central East Africa.

The conclusion that Muller draws from this evidence is: 'The ancient Egyptian Afterlife Paradise was called the Tuat. It was imagined to be a place of lakes and mountains like East Africa. The Egyptians knew these places because they originated in this region and called it Place of the First Time.'

Which ever be the case, the dead person (or Manes) travelled through the Netherworld on foot or by boat using *heka* to open pathways and to banish darkness. Overcoming pathlessness and darkness reflected the idea in the creation story of order triumphing over disorder as in Ma'at versus Isfet. The dead person was now on a voyage to dwell in the kingdom of Osiris, travel through the Duat with Ra, or enter the Fields of Reeds.

Gerald Massey pictures the Manes as a pilgrim armed with his *Book of the Dead,* journeying through Amenta. Holding on to the roll is specifically mentioned in Chapter 15. To get to these locations, the dead person must negotiate the challenges faced by the gates, the mounds, and the caverns. He must also avoid the punishments reserved for the unrighteous.

However, the numbers, locations, and guards to be negotiated of the gates, mounds, and caverns differs from papyri to papyri. According to Walter Marsham Adams:

> [F]rom several allusions in the writings, we find that the efficacy attached to them arose from the deceased having been permitted to become acquainted with them during lifetime, so that the papyrus attested the instruction in Wisdom of which the departed possessed at death.

This explains why each papyrus was different.

The gates could be seen as providing a protective ring around the kingdom of Osiris. To pass through these gates one had to get past frightening divine beings armed with knives. Each gate had its keeper, its guard, and its announcer. All three must be successfully negotiated.

You could only pass by correctly uttering the names of the deities and uttering the names of the gates. As an example, Chapter 144 says:

> [M]ake way for me, for I know you, I know your name, and I know the name of the god who guards you. 'Mistress of Darkness,' ... its height cannot be known from its breadth, and its extent in space cannot be discovered. Snakes are on it, of which the number is not known, it was fashioned before the 'Inert One' is your name. 'He who was joined together' is the name of her door-keeper.

Other guards had names such as 'who hacks up the human dead' or 'who dances in blood' or 'sharp of knife against the talker.'

The same idea existed in the world of the living. Professor Taylor makes some interesting claims:

The content of these spells bring to mind the layout of Egyptian temples ... the temple sanctuary in which the god dwelt was surrounded by numerous walls pierced with gateways, as may still be seen at Karnak, and each gateway was guarded by an attendant. The priests, in order to enter and perform their duties in the temples, had to pass an initiation involved in the demonstration of their purity and special knowledge. The texts for some of these procedures survive and display close affinities with passages from the Book of the Dead.

Walter Marsham Adams calls the papyrus roll *'The Book of the Master of the Hidden Places'* to emphasise that he also sees an analogy between the *Book of the Dead* and the inside of an initiation temple. The only difference is that he thinks it refers to the inside of the Great Pyramid and not Karnak. Incidentally, both Massey and Adams portray the journey in the *Book of the Dead* as one long series of trials or ordeals.

All of this strongly demonstrates how much the Freemasons have copied from the ancient Egyptians.

It was also important to negotiate the mounds. The mounds were important for two reasons. Firstly, they existed in the Egyptian (and Central African) landscape. Secondly, they represented the deity Ptah emerging from the watery abyss of Nun as in the creation story.

How do you negotiate the mounds?

Chapter 149 says:

The fourth mount: green ... The deceased says: 'As for the chief of the mysterious mound, as for the very high mountain, which is in the realm of the dead, in which the sky sets, it is 300 rods long by 150 rods wide; a snake is on it called 'Castor of knives', and it is 70 cubits when it glides; it lives by decapitating the spirits of the dead in the realm of the dead. I rise up against you [a snake], so that navigation may be carried out aright; I have seen the way to you and I will gather myself together against you, for I am the male. Cover your head, for I am hale, hale, I am one mighty of magic, and my eyes have caused me to benefit therefrom ...'

The dead person would also have to negotiate caverns. Each cavern was occupied by one or more divine beings. The dead person also had to know about other beings that existed in the Netherworld. There were the souls of the East, the souls of the West, and the souls of the cities of Heliopolis, Hermopolis, Nekhen, and Pe.

Chapter 17 represents the passage of the deceased as playing *senet,* which literally means passage or passing. The idea was in some way connected to the passage of the sun through the underworld which was similar to the passage of the *ba* at night giving new life to the mummy.

Figure 7. Ani playing senet from the *Papyrus of Ani*. What does this game of *senet* look like to you?

In the realm of Amenta it was important that the Manes had *heka,* not just to negotiate the gates, mounds, caverns and other beings, but also to preserve their physical body, including the head and heart. Chapter 27 speaks of a divine power 'who seize hearts' and can therefore turn your heart against you in the judgement scene.

It was also important to protect the *ka* just in case the relatives did not supply the correct offerings. Chapter 105 freed the dead person from dependence on their relatives and priests as long as he or she wore the correct papyrus around their necks. Professor Taylor says:

> The illusion is to the practice of wearing around the neck a small roll of papyrus
> inscribed with a protective text.

I believe this can be compared with other African practices. To give an example, there is a famous painting of Ayuba Suleiman Diallo (also known as Job ben Solomon) from 1733. In this case he has a Qur'an around his neck.

Figure 8. 1733 painting of Ayuba Suleiman Diallo.

Chapter 61 protected the *ba* from being taken from its owner. Chapters 91, 92 and 188 protected the *shut* or shadow. If all of these elements of the self were successfully reunited, the person became an effective and justified spirit or an *akh*.

Chapters 76 to 88 were transformation spells allowing the Manes to become a falcon, a heron, a swallow, a snake, a crocodile, a lotus flower, or any form he wishes. These forms were important in the dead person moving from the Netherworld to the realm of the living.

I raise the question: Is this where certain later religions took their ideas of reincarnation in the form of animals?

Another set of challenges that the dead person had to negotiate were dangerous animals such as crocodiles and snakes including Apep the great enemy of Ra. Chapter 31 says against the crocodile:

> Get back! Retreat! Get back, you dangerous one! Do not come against me, do not live by my magic; May I not have to tell this name of yours to the Great God who sent you.

In the Egyptian belief system, Apep battles nightly against Ra who is trying to rise on the eastern horizon with Apep trying to prevent this.

Yet another form of danger the dead individual had to avoid was the punishment of the unjustified. Many of these punishments were at the command of Osiris. These involved avoiding slaughter, putrefaction, having your rightful place taken, dying a second death, traps such as the fishing net and the world turning upside down. This last form of danger would involve, among other things, your digestive system working the wrong way round and thus the victim drank urine and ate faeces. There was the danger of drinking burning water and your supply of air failing. Again, there were utterances protecting the dead individual from these consequences.

Summing up

Despite the very different approaches given by Gerald Massey and John Taylor, they paint a remarkably similar picture. There were gates, mounds, caverns and their fearsome guardians. There were other spiritual beings, turquoise trees, iron walls, lakes of fire, traps and the world upside down. There were evil-minded divine beings and evil-minded serpents.

Against this was the pilgrim armed with his papyrus roll and divine protection because of his knowledge of the secrets, rituals and the words of power.

I suggest that the *Book of the Dead* is the original template for ALL adventure stories from *Jason and the Golden Fleece* of the ancient Greek period, to *Harry Potter* today. This gives substance to Major General Forlong's claim that:

Figure 9. Battling Apep in the form of a python. Is this the origin of the St George and the Dragon iconography?

It was undoubtedly Kushites who rendered possible the Aryan advance, and who played the part of a civilizing Rome thousands of years before Roma's birth. It was their vast mythology and strange legends that passed as Lord Bacon wrote "like light air into the flutes of Grecians, there to be modulated as best suited Grecian fancies." Indeed, it is manifest from many old writings, that it was their tales, myths, traditions and histories that lay at base of the Western World's thought and legendary lore. These so impressed all subsequent races and entered so deeply and minutely into all Aryan mythologies that many writers now think Aryans can only claim to have added to the superstructure and complexion of Ethiopian myths and mythical history.

CHAPTER SIX: IN THE HALL OF THE TWO MA'ATS

The greatest challenge to the dead individual was the judgement. This is where there was a review of the person's whole life carried out in the presence of Osiris involving the weighing of the heart. It was at this point the Manes was judged whether or not he was worthy to be an immortal. The justified were rewarded but the unjustified were punished. The dead person proved his worthiness by his demonstration of the special knowledge needed to pass through the gates and repel dangerous animals.

From the time of Egyptian Dynasty V, texts were written on good conduct. This involved maintaining the balance of society, showing reverence to the divine forces, supporting the less fortunate, and observing ritual practices. All of this could be summed up as 'Ma'at'. The righteous would also have had to have made the words of Osiris truth against his enemies.

However, Professor Taylor claims:

> There is no Egyptian equivalent of the Bible's Ten Commandments, in which proper conduct is laid down by divine word.

In my opinion, his British Museum catalogue is excellent, but … let me leave it at that! I do agree, however, with the following statement:

> These texts do not present a collective 'day of judgement' for all humanity, as in Christian doctrine, but the single episode undergone by each individual during the passage from life to the afterlife.

This also suggests that life is cyclical and the world is not coming to an end any time soon.

Chapter 125 says:

> This is the way to act in the Hall of the two Ma'ats. A man says this speech when he is pure, clean, dressed in fresh clothes, shod in white sandals, painted with eye paint, anointed with the finest oil or myrrh.

To enter the Hall, the individual had to answer questions posed by the divine beings on who he is, and the Mysteries of Osiris. Following this, he

Fig 10. Osiris sitting in judgement from the *Papyrus of Hunefer.*

is invited to enter. He is then asked to name the individual components of the doorway. He then enters and is announced to Thoth, the deity that acts as a messenger and a guide. The conversation is as follows:

'Why have you come?'
'To be announced.'
'What is your condition?'
'I am free of every sin.'
'To whom shall I announce you?
'To him whose ceiling is fire, whose walls are living uraeii, whose house floor is the flood.'
'Who is that?'
'Osiris.'

Osiris sits in judgement, often attended by Isis, Nepthys, and the four sons of Horus. The dead person declared that he was innocent of various sins before Osiris. He then made 42 declarations of innocence before the 42 divine beings also in judgement.

Firstly, the dead person addressed Osiris as follows:

> Praise be to thee, thou great god, thou lord of the two truths ... I come to thee and bring thee truth, and chase away wrong doing. I have committed no sins against mankind ... I have not done that which the gods abhor. I have made no man evil in the eyes of his superior. I have not caused to hunger. I have not caused to weep. I have done no murder. I have not commanded to murder. I have not occasioned grief to any ...

The other sins avoided by the justified were fraud in trade, stealing milk from children, stealing and injuring cattle, snaring sacred birds, fishing in lakes, diverting the Nile flood water and stealing from the sacred temples.

Secondly, the dead person addressed each of the 42 judges as follows:

> Far-strider who came forth from Heliopolis, I have done no falsehood. Fire-embracer who came forth Kheraha, I have not robbed. Swallow of shades who came forth from the cavern, I have not stolen. Dangerous one who came forth from Rosetjau, I have not killed men. Flame which came forth backwards, I have not stolen the god's offerings. Bone breaker who came forth from Heracleopolis, I have not told lies.

There are, of course, 36 others. As a whole, the declarations forbid injury to the sacred and the dead, murder, oppression, theft, robbing minors, fraud, impurity, adultery, lying, slander, reviling, and eavesdropping. Professor Adolf Erman adds:

> [A]ll of which are also condemned in our scheme of morality. There is only one which exceeds ours, the remarkable but fine command which forbids heart eating, i.e. useless remorse.

I add that we need to challenge this notion of 'command' cf. commandment. The *Book of the Dead* is about the individual taking responsibility for doing Ma'at. It is not about being COMMANDED by a superior force to do good. I add that this too exceeds 'our scheme of morality.'

What were the implications of Chapter 125 for everyday life?

The *Declaration of Virtues* were obituary texts that began to be written in the Old Kingdom and evolved into Chapter 125. One such example reads as follows:

> I gave bread to the hungry and clothes to the naked, and gave a passage in my own boat to those who could not cross. I was a father to the orphan, a husband to the widow, a protection from the wind to the shivering; I am one who spake what was good and related what was good (not a scandal monger). I acquired my possessions in a just manner.

Professor Maulana Karenga presents the *Declaration of Virtues* along with other texts and the *Book of the Dead* as presenting a moral IDEAL for everyday life. In a Cambridge museum lecture, he explained the dangers, possibilities and limitations of judging a society by its documented ideals since ideals often contradict the reality e.g. The American Constitution. The point is the Egyptians ASPIRED to live up to these high ideals.

Following this was the Weighing of the Heart. In one pan was placed the heart, in the other pan was placed an ostrich feather (which represents Ma'at). The heart should be as light as the feather. This symbolised that the individual was virtuous and guiltless (i.e. he did not have a heavy heart).

There were, however, attempts to lower the ethical standards. Professor Taylor makes the following revealing statement:

> The demotic story of Setne gives a slightly different picture, in which the weight of one's good and bad deeds is compared, the result determining one's future state, but this is a very late source and may reflect influence from the Graeco-Roman world.

Make of that what you will!

Figure 11. Weighing of the Heart from the *Papyrus of Ani.*

However, the Egyptians themselves were not entirely above nonsense. They believed that the heart could give them away and reveal information that was damaging in the Judgement Hall. Consequently, Chapter 30 B says:

> O my heart of my mother! ... Do not stand up as a witness against me, do not be opposed to me in the tribunal, do not be hostile to me in the presence of the Keeper of the Balance.

If things went well, the following occurred. Thoth says:

> I have judged the heart of the deceased, and his soul stands as a witness for him. His deeds are righteous in the great balance, and no sin has been found in him.

Horus then presents the deceased to Osiris. Finally, the individual says:

> Here I am in your presence, or Lord of the West. There is no wrongdoing in my body, I have not wittingly told lies, there has been no second fault. Grant that I may be like the favoured ones ... O Osiris, one greatly favoured by the good god, one loved of the Lord of the two lands, the deceased, vindicated before Osiris.

If things went badly, the individual faced the Devourer, also called the Devourer of 'the Unjustified' or 'the Damned,' or the Devourer who destroys 'enemies'. She is also called the Lady of the Duat or the Devourer of the West. This female being had the rear of a hippopotamus, the front half and forelegs of a lion, and the head of crocodile. Those who faced the Devourer became the twice dead or the *mutu*.

What else could happen?

The *Books of the Netherworld* portray the unjustified burning in fiery furnaces, being decapitated or being dismembered. Professor Taylor says that the fiery furnaces 'seem to prefigure early Christian notions of hell.'

One late period text suggests that a man be judged 'according to the measure of his term of life that Thoth wrote for him'. Professor Taylor suggests this means predestination. I suggest that this idea is the precursor to Judaism's Book of Life concept where an individual's life (and its successes and failures) has already been mapped out for them and pre-written by God.

The individual who successfully passed through the Hall of the two Ma'ats now became one of the *maa-kheru* i.e. true of voice. The successful

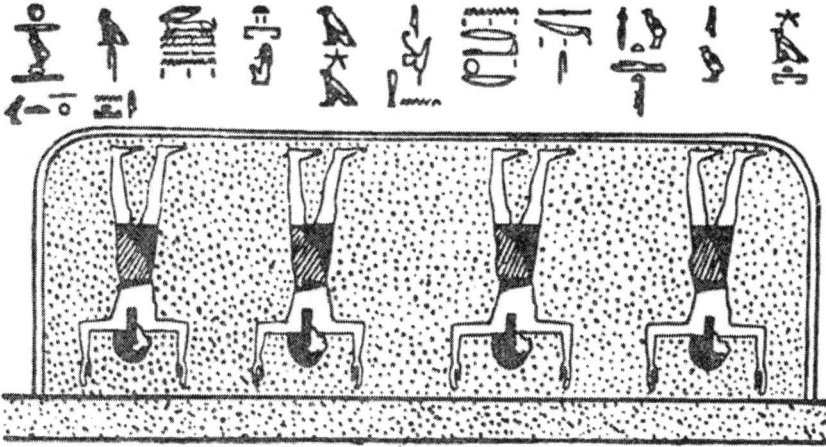

Figure 12. The damned cast downwards into the pit of fire.

individual has their heart returned and they stand with arms raised in an attitude of joy. They are sometimes supported by Ma'at and are adorned with feathers.

Once vindicated, one objective was to become one with Ra and travel in his solar boat. Chapters 100 and 102 allow the individual to navigate that boat and drive away the hostile serpent Apep.

Another objective was to enter the Field of Reeds. This was perhaps located somewhere in the East, where Ra began his morning journey. It was a place where the deities and the justified lived forever in contentment and peace. The landscape had waterways, fields, and abundant crops.

Is there a description of the Fields of Reeds?

Chapters 109 and 149 claim that:

> Its walls are of iron, its barley stands five cubits high, with ears of two stalks of three cubits, And its wheat stand seven cubits high, with ears of three and stalks of four cubits; it is the blessed, each of them 9 cubits tall, who reap them alongside the Eastern Souls.

The ancient Greek idea of the Elysian Fields was derived from the Egyptian Field of Reeds. However, these fields still had to be worked by someone. Chapter 6 says:

> O shabti allotted to me, if I be summoned or if I be detailed to do any work which has to be done in the realm of the dead ... you shall detail yourself for

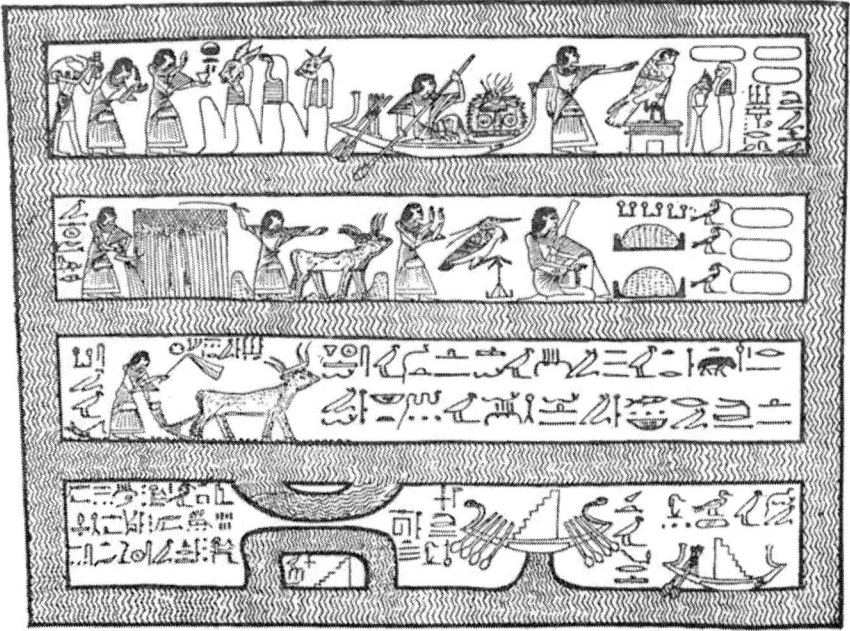

Figure 13. The Field of Reeds from the *Papyrus of Ani*.

me on every occasion of making arable fields, flooding the banks or of conveying sand from east to west; 'Here I am,' you shall say.

This essentially meant that a shabti could do the work for you. In the early days, these shabtis were personalised doubles of you. In later times, they became 'ushebtis' standardised and impersonal, and acting as your servants or slaves.

CONCLUSIONS

The *Book of the Dead* is a body of writings of the very greatest significance.

Its chapters reflect and elaborate on the oldest recorded theological system in the world dating back to Egyptian Dynasty V, if not earlier. Its presentation in black and red ink (and sometimes blue ink) uses the primary colours that printers use today. The theological ideas themselves show similarities to those believed and practised elsewhere in Africa.. The imagery in those scriptures came from Central East Africa. Other Egyptian theological ideas were borrowed by the later religions of India and the Greeks. Other ideas were borrowed by the great traditions of Judaism and Christianity.

Figure 14. These images indicate that it was not just Judaism and Christianity that were influenced by the *Book of the Dead.*

The *Book of the Dead* is also the template for all later adventure stories from the time of the ancient Greeks right up the *Harry Potter* era.

Even the board games of drafts and chess have their beginnings in the *Book of the Dead*.

BIBLIOGRAPHY

Main Source

John H. Taylor, *Ancient Egyptian Book of the Dead*, UK, The British Museum Press, 2010

Others

W. Marsham Adams, *The Book of the Master*, 1898, reprint US, ECA Associates, 1990

Yosef A. A. Ben-Jochannan, *Africa! Mother of Western Civilization*, US, Black Classic Press, 1971

E. A. Wallis Budge, *Egyptian Ideas of the Future Life*, 1900, reprinted as *Egyptian Religion*, USA, Kensington Press, 1997

E. A. Wallis Budge, *The Book of the Dead*, 1913, reprint US, University Books, 1960

Adolf Erman, *A Handbook of Egyptian Religion*, UK, Richard Clay & Sons, 1907

Charles Finch, *Echoes of the Old Darkland*, US, Khenti, 1991

Major General J. G. R. Forlong, *Rivers of Life, Volume 2*, UK, Bernard Quaritch, 1883

Maulana Karenga, *MAAT: The Moral Ideal in Ancient Egypt*, US, University of Sankore Press, 2006

Gerald Massey, *Ancient Egypt: The Light of the World, Volume 1*, UK, S. P. C. K., 1907

Gert Muller, *East African and Nubian Origins of the Ancient Egyptians,* UK, Pomegranate Publishing, 2013

David Rankine, *Heka,* UK, Avalonia, 2006

PART FOUR

THE AUTHOR

ROBIN WALKER

Biography

Robin Walker 'The Black History Man' was born in London but has also lived in Jamaica. He attended the London School of Economics and Political Science where he read Economics.

In 1991 and 1992, he studied African World Studies with the brilliant Dr Femi Biko and later with Mr Kenny Bakie. Between 1993 and 1994, he trained as a secondary school teacher at Edge Hill College (linked to the University of Lancaster).

Since 1992 and up to the present period, Robin Walker has lectured in adult education, taught university short courses, and chaired conferences in African World Studies, Egyptology and Black History. The venues have been in Toxteth (Liverpool), Manchester, Leeds, Bradford, Huddersfield, Birmingham, Cambridge, Buckinghamshire and London.

Since 1994 he has taught Economics, Business & Finance, Mathematics, Information Communications Technology, PSHE/Citizenship and also History at various schools in London and Essex.

In 1999 he wrote *Classical Splendour: Roots of Black History* published in the UK by Bogle L'Ouverture Publications. In the same year, he co-authored (with Siaf Millar) *The West African Empire of Songhai,* a textbook used by many schools across the country.

In 2000 he co-authored (again with Siaf Millar) *Sword, Seal and Koran,* another book on the Songhai Empire of West Africa.

In 2006 he wrote the seminal *When We Ruled.* This was the most advanced synthesis on Ancient and Mediaeval African history ever written by a single author. It was a massive expansion of his earlier book *Classical Splendour: Roots of Black History* and established his reputation as the leading Black History educational service provider.

In 2008 he wrote *Before The Slave Trade,* a highly pictorial companion volume to *When We Ruled.*

Between 2011 and 2014 he wrote a series of e-books for download sold through Amazon Kindle. These e-books covered history, business, religion, music, and science.

In 2013, he co-authored (with Siaf Millar and Saran Keita) *Everyday Life In An Early West African Empire*. It was a massive expansion on the earlier book *Sword, Seal & Koran*. He updated *When We Ruled* by incorporating nearly all of the images from *Before The Slave Trade*. He wrote a trilogy of books entitled *Blacks and Science Volumes One, Two* and *Three*.

In 2014, he wrote *The Rise and Fall of Black Wall Street and the Seven Key Empowerment Principles*. He also wrote the book that you are holding right now *Blacks and Religion Volume One*.

Speaking Engagements

Looking for a speaker for your next event?

The author Robin Walker 'The Black History Man' is dynamic and engaging, both as a speaker and a workshop leader. He brings Black or African history alive, making it relevant for the present generation. You will love his perfect blend of accessibility, engagement, and academic rigour where learning becomes fun.

Walker is available to give speaking engagements to a variety of audiences.

Motivational crowds, general audiences, schools and parents will enjoy Walker's highly engaging presentation *From Africa to the World: The Evolution of the Concept of Self and the Changing Uses of Psychology*. Academic crowds will enjoy his *What did Africa Contribute to Religion?*

To book Robin Walker for your next event, send an email to historicalwalker@yahoo.com

INDEX

31878681R00071

Made in the USA
Charleston, SC
31 July 2014